TO:
CHRISTOPHER JOHNSON, MD

D1563293

DAVID PRINCE

PIONEER SURGEON

Robert Berry

Robert Berry (signature)

BookLocker
Saint Petersburg, Florida

ISBN: 978-1-64719-488-8

Published by BookLocker.com, Inc., St. Petersburg, Florida.

Printed on acid-free paper.

BookLocker.com, Inc.
2021

First Edition

COVER: *Source: Courtesy of Illinois College Schewe Library Archives. The Club Literary Society file.*

Library of Congress Cataloging in Publication Data
Berry, Robert
David Prince: Pioneer Surgeon by Robert Berry
Library of Congress Control Number: 2021905330

Disclaimer

This book content details does not include any of the author's personal experiences with medicine and does not offer medical advice. The author is not a healthcare provider.

The author and publisher are providing this book and its contents on an "as is" basis and make no representations or warranties of any kind with respect to this book or its contents. The author and publisher disclaim all such representations and warranties, including for example warranties of merchantability and healthcare for a particular purpose. In addition, the author and publisher do not represent or warrant that the information accessible via this book is accurate, complete or current.

The statements made about products and services have not been evaluated by the U.S. Food and Drug Administration. They are not intended to diagnose, treat, cure, or prevent any condition or disease. Please consult with your own physician or healthcare specialist regarding the suggestions and recommendations made in this book.

Except as specifically stated in this book, neither the author or publisher, nor any authors, contributors, or other representatives will be liable for damages arising out of or in connection with the use of this book. This is a comprehensive limitation of liability that applies to all damages of any kind, including (without limitation) compensatory; direct, indirect or consequential damages; loss of data, income or profit; loss of or damage to property and claims of third parties.

You understand that this book is not intended as a substitute for consultation with a licensed healthcare practitioner, such as your physician. Before you begin any healthcare program, or change your lifestyle in any way, you will consult your physician or other licensed healthcare practitioner to ensure that you are in good health and that the examples contained in this book will not harm you.

This book provides content related to topics physical and/or mental health issues. As such, use of this book implies your acceptance of this disclaimer.

Dedication

Dedicated to my Wisconsin kidney donor – January 2011.

Acknowledgements

Thanks to my editor Mike Kienzler; Susan Rishworth, Archivist, American College of Surgeons in Chicago for her generosity of time and arranging return of seventy-one rare books to Illinois College that had been part of a donation in 1940 to ACS by the Morgan County Medical Society; Chris Ashmore, Director, Jacksonville IL Public Library; Director Luke Beatty, and Archivist Samantha Sauer, Schewe Library, Illinois College; Robert Cavanaugh, Abraham Lincoln Presidential Library, Springfield, IL; Jared Scarborough, Payson, Illinois, Scarborough Family Papers; The Newberry Library, Chicago; University of Illinois Chicago, Health Sciences Special Collection; Herman B. Wells Library, Indiana University; and the support of Kathleen Roegge and Emily Berry Morris.

Table of Contents

Preface

This biography of pioneer surgeon Dr. David Prince (1816-1889) began while I was researching for material on a biography of the internationally recognized dentist Dr. Greene Vardiman Black from Jacksonville, Illinois. I quickly found Black had already been the subject of several published biographies. However, there had been no previous book-length biographies of Prince, who collaborated closely with Black in the development of innovative methods and instruments for the repair of a cleft palate. Further investigation convinced me that, beyond his work with Black, Prince's career is worthy of its own biography which includes his pioneering work in plastic surgery and orthopedics.

Considerable primary source material is available in the papers of Prince's contemporaries held by the Abraham Lincoln Presidential Library in Springfield, Illinois. Some of Prince's own papers are contained in the papers of Dr. Carl E. Black. Carl Black, the son of G.V. Black, was a student of Prince before attending medical school.

Internet sites show Prince published more than one hundred articles in medical journals on a wide variety of topics. Most of his writing came after the Civil War, beginning in 1866 and continuing until a few months before his death in 1889. Highlights of Prince's publications include his reports to the United States Sanitary Commission during and after the Peninsula Campaign of the Civil War. His reports are based on the diary he kept during the war. The reports include twenty-four days he spent as a volunteer prisoner/physician in the Libby Prison in Richmond, Virginia.

David Prince, Pioneer Surgeon is set against historical events in the growth of Jacksonville, Illinois, where Prince spent his most productive years.

Robert Berry
January 2021

I
Fairfield Medical School

"It is creditable to the professors of Fairfield, several of whom are not unknown to fame, that they are able in a village to attract larger classes than their brethren of the great city, who have over them so many natural and statistical advantages."
The Western Journal, 1837

David Prince, as an adult, was of short stature "with a head that was large in proportion to his body and had an open countenance." He is described as "remarkably strong and rugged." Known to be blunt and direct, he was also approachable by patients and students as well as by other physicians. He was active in community affairs and had a deep interest in politics at the local, state and national levels. These characteristics are reflective of the people close to him, beginning with his father, David Prince Sr., and later his mentor Reuben Mussey.[1]

More is known about Prince's medical education than his early preparation. His father was a farmer in Brooklyn, Connecticut when David Jr., the first of six children, was born in 1816. The family's New England history is traced to 1662. David Prince was at least the seventh in his family to be given that name. His mother, Sophia Ellsworth Prince, was a relative of William W. Ellsworth, who served as governor of Connecticut from 1838 to 1842. David's youngest brother, Edward, born in 1832, served with distinction as a lieutenant colonel in the Seventh Illinois Cavalry during the Civil War. Edward was inspired perhaps by his grandfather, Maj. Timothy Prince, who served in the Revolutionary War.[2]

The family moved before David's fourth birthday to Bloomfield, New York, twenty-four miles southeast of Rochester in the Finger Lakes district. Western New York was a popular destination for many Connecticut families seeking better lives. They named several villages after ones they left in Connecticut. Prince received a high school education at Canandaigua Academy, a private school for boys founded in 1791 near Bloomfield. He attended classes in the winter and worked on his father's farm the rest of the year.[3]

Prince was nineteen when he graduated from the academy in 1835. His father decided that year to move farther west, relocating in Payson, Illinois, about twenty miles southeast of Quincy. Members of Sophia Prince's extended family had settled in Payson previously. Preparations for the move included loading a wagon with merchandise to sell when his father would open the first dry goods store in Payson.

David Prince Jr. did not leave with his family. He decided to pursue a career in medicine and enrolled in the College of Physicians and Surgeons of the Western District of New York in Fairfield, east of Utica. The school was commonly referred to as the Fairfield Medical School. At the time, Fairfield Medical School terms lasted twelve weeks each. The school charged students $157 for a room, $1.25 a week for board and $7 for use of the library. Research reveals few details of Prince's financial arrangements, except that he did odd jobs in the summer and received aid from a family friend when he moved to Fairfield. He also may have qualified for the school's policy of accepting indigent students. Prince spent two years at Fairfield, but left before graduating to follow Dr. Reuben Mussey to the Medical College of Ohio in Cincinnati.[4]

A Prince biographer characterized him as having wide interests and being widely read. A book from his extensive personal library is inscribed on the front page: "D. Prince, Jr. Fairfield Oct 1836." The book by Baron Dominique Jean Larrey (1766-1842) is *Observations on Wounds, and Their Complications by Erysipelas, Gangrene and Tetanus, and on the Principal Diseases and Injuries of the Head, Ear, and Eye.* The English translation was published in Philadelphia in 1832. Baron Larrey, a close friend of Napoleon, served in the Napoleonic Wars as chief surgeon of the Grand Army. The text gives detailed descriptions of a variety of surgical procedures in hospitals and on battlefields. Larrey is noted for creating a system of ambulances and moveable hospitals where he and his assistant surgeons performed operations. Especially noted is his belief that lives could be saved by performing amputations on the battlefield in the heat of battle, instead of waiting for the battle to be over to tend the wounded.[5]

In the first chapter of *Observations on Wounds,* focusing on gunshot wounds, Larrey describes his justification: "I never, from the first commencement of the hostilities of that war, dreaded to carry the comforts of my art in the midst of the combatants. It was then that I created those light, itinerant hospitals, which have so much reduced the number of victims to the deadly blows of the fatal sisters; and it was then, also, on the fields of glory and carnage, if I may venture thus to express myself, that I became convinced of the necessity of operating, immediately, upon those whose limbs had been mutilated or destroyed by projectile weapons."[6]

Fairfield Medical School began to confer medical degrees when it was chartered in 1812. Enrollment grew, and the school attracted talented physicians, many from New England. Among the notable professors when Prince attended, in addition to Mussey, were Lyman Spalding, George Shattuck, John Delamater and Frank Hamilton, later a U.S. medical inspector who specialized in fractures. Fairfield graduates were in demand as the western population grew. At the same time, the faculty was being recruited by other schools.[7]

Spalding was widely known for his abilities as a physician, surgeon, lecturer and teacher. He led the convention that released the first publication of *United States Pharmacopeia* (1820). His presence on the faculty was important for recruitment. Spalding stressed the importance of dissection as essential to the study of anatomy and surgery. Josiah Noyes, Fairfield's distinguished professor of chemistry, mineralogy and materia medica, recruited Spalding in a letter dated October 2, 1810 wherein he described the academy's medical department and proposed school of medicine:

> *The number of students besides Medical Students is generally from 90 to 115. It is expected that the Academy and Medical Institution connected will take the name of College soon. The instruction at present is about the same as is given in the most respectable college in the United States. There is, besides, one Tutor and an assistant who attends to the lower branches. We have three buildings, one of stone called the Laboratory, containing 14 elegant rooms. There are two lecturing rooms, one for Anatomy, and another for lectures on Chemistry. These two rooms perhaps are better than any others built for the same purpose in the United States, except Philadelphia. Our Chemical Apparatus is more complete than any in the City of New York, and*

the Anatomical Museum is equal to Nathan Smith's at Dartmouth.[8]

Prince's professional interest in dissection first developed at Fairfield. Spalding, distinguished professor of anatomy and surgery, had been a student and colleague of Dartmouth Medical School founder Nathan Smith. Smith taught that experience was more important than theory in the study of anatomy. As a result, dissection became a focus of anatomy classes at Fairfield. In an 1816 letter Spalding mentioned he had performed fourteen dissections during the previous school year.[9]

As with all medical schools in the eighteenth and nineteenth centuries, Fairfield had difficulties from time to time getting "subjects" for dissection. Instructors usually were responsible for procurement, but Fairfield also employed an administrator to supply bodies for dissection. The school's policy held that students could not obtain dissecting material without the administrator's approval. Nevertheless, enterprising students were known to engage in grave robbing that had dangers beyond sparking the anger of families and the community. On one occasion, some students contracted smallpox from a cadaver whose death apparently was caused by the disease. In 1826, Fairfield was granted permission by the New York legislature to obtain the bodies of executed criminals from Auburn State Prison. That arrangement was ended in 1833 because of political machinations by competing medical schools.[10]

By the time Prince enrolled in 1836, Fairfield's winter term had been reduced to twelve weeks, and dissection material was in short supply. At Fairfield, Prince became acquainted with two students who became lifelong friends and colleagues: Nathan Smith Davis, who was involved in organizing Northwestern University Medical School, and Daniel Brainard, who started Rush Medical College in Chicago. All three were involved with establishing the Illinois State Medical Society. They helped lead the effort to establish legal ways for medical schools in Illinois to obtain cadavers. They also sought legislation to license Illinois physicians who graduated from chartered medical schools to set them apart from quacks.

Fairfield Medical School closed in 1841, merging partly with Albany Medical College and partly with Geneva Medical College. Fairfield had given instruction to 3,123 students and graduated 589. The last class numbered 164, thirty of whom were graduates.[11]

Prince had already moved on. While at Fairfield, Prince became impressed with Mussey, who at the time was professor of anatomy and surgery. Prince followed Mussey when Mussey left in 1837 to teach at the Medical College of Ohio in Cincinnati.

Prince visited his parents in Illinois before entering the Ohio school. Prince's cousin, Philo Thompson, mentioned Prince's visit to Payson in a letter to his brother Samuel Thompson in Connecticut: "Dr. David Prince is here practicing his profession, makes himself quite useful – no other physician in the place – he is really a fine young man."[12]

A year later, Prince's sister Mary wrote to her cousin (Philo's sister Emily) in Connecticut: "Brother David is going to start for Cincinnati tomorrow to spend six months. He has very good success here. We shall miss him very much so. There is no Physician in this place at present – it has been rather unhealthy during the warm season."[13]

ENDNOTES

[1] Norbury, Frank, M.D. "David Prince/ A Pioneer in Surgical Therapeutics in Central Illinois." 11; Jacksonville Courier. December 20, 1889.

[2] Campbell, John C. *A biographical history, with portraits, of prominent men of the great West.* Chicago. 114-115.

[3] Norbury, Frank, M.D. "David Prince." *Illinois Medical Journal.* May 1966. 1.

[4] Black, Ardeen. "A Pioneer Surgeon." Unpublished; O'Donnell, Thomas C. *Tip of the Hill.* Booneville, NY. Black River Books. 1953. 130.

[5] Ross, J. C., M.D., M.CH. "Napoleon's Chief Surgeon and His Times." *The Ulster Medical Journal.* 104.

[6] Larrey, Baron Dominique Jean. Observations on Wounds, and Their Complications by Erysipelas, Gangrene and Tetanus, and on the Principal Diseases and Injuries of the Head, Ear, and Eye. Philadelphia. 1832. 1. This book is the first of three volumes under the title of Clinque Chirurgicale, published in Paris from 1829-1830. It is one of the seventy-one books returned to Illinois College in 2013 from the 1941 donation to the American College of Surgeons by the Morgan County Medical Society.

[7] O'Donnell. *Tip of the Hill.* 50-58.

[8] Spalding, Dr. James Alfred. *Dr. Lyman Spalding.* Boston. W.M. Leonard, Publisher. 1916 195.

[9] Spalding, James. 241.

[10] Spalding, James. 238. Letter from Willoughby to Spalding, Jan 27, 1816; O'Donnell. *Tip of the Hill.* 111, 241.

[11] Spalding, James. 242; Polk's Medical Register and Directory of North America. 1914-1915 Thirteenth Revised Edition. Publisher: R. L. Polk & Co., Publishers-Detroit, New York, Chicago. Copyright: 1914.

---

[12] Philo Thompson to Samuel Thompson. September 20, 1837. Scarborough, Jared. Payson, Illinois. Family papers and letters. David Prince was related to the Scarborough family through his mother's aunt, who married into the Scarborough family.

[13] Mary Prince to Emily Thompson. September 1838. Jared Scarborough Family papers and letters.

II
Prince's Mentor

"Observe the coincidences between certain great political and intellectual periods and the appearance of illustrious medical reformers and teachers."
Oliver Wendell Holmes Sr., M.D., 1861

When David Prince and Reuben Mussey arrived in 1837, Cincinnati, with more than 45,000 people, was the sixth largest city in the nation and largest in the West. Its foreign-born populace, which was large, included many cultivated men and women. According to Dr. Daniel Drake, they came in pursuit of fortune "not so much to cultivate literature as commerce and more interested in establishments for manufacturing than for scientific study."[1]

Abolitionism was the primary public excitement. Abolitionist sentiments had been growing in Cincinnati all through the 1830s, peaking in July 1836, when the offices of the anti-slavery weekly *The Philanthropist,* published by James Birney, was mobbed and destroyed by several hundred men instigated by Kentucky slave owners.[2]

In 1837, national figures visited Cincinnati and the home of Gen. William Henry Harrison in nearby North Bend prior to his election to the Presidency in 1840. In the summer, Daniel Webster, U.S. senator from Massachusetts, was a guest of the city during his western tour. Harrison introduced Webster to an assemblage. A grand reception was held for President Andrew

Jackson in October. Jackson had left his presidency in March and was on his way to the Hermitage accompanied by future president James K. Polk and his wife.[3]

In the 1830s, Cincinnati's luminaries included abolitionist Rev. Lyman Beecher, president of Lane Theological Seminary, Rev. Calvin Ellis Stowe and his wife Harriet Beecher Stowe, later the author of *Uncle Tom's Cabin*. The president of Cincinnati College was Rev. W.H. McGuffey, the author/editor of the original McGuffey Readers series of reading primers for elementary school students. These leaders and others attended Dr. Daniel Drake's bi-monthly literary circle, including a young Salmon P. Chase, who went on to be governor of Ohio, Abraham Lincoln's secretary of the treasury and the sixth chief justice of the United States Supreme Court.[4]

David Prince had connections with the Beecher family before and after his time in Cincinnati. The Prince family lived in Litchfield, Connecticut when Lyman Beecher was minister of the Congregational Church there from 1810 to 1826. Prince likely was baptized by Beecher; however, the early records of the First Congregational Church of Litchfield were lost in a fire. When Prince was appointed professor of anatomy and surgery for the Illinois College Medical Department in Jacksonville, Illinois, in 1843, the president of Illinois College was Edward Beecher, son of Lyman Beecher and the brother of Harriet Beecher Stowe and Henry Ward Beecher. (These associations account, in part, for Prince's participation in the Underground Railroad when he lived and practiced in Jacksonville.)

Prince and Mussey arrived in Cincinnati in the autumn of 1837 to prepare for the new session of the Medical College of Ohio. They entered a school that had two decades of turmoil involving personal and professional jealousies, frequent faculty turnover and animosity toward the founder, Daniel Drake.

In 1818, Drake successfully petitioned the Ohio legislature for a charter to operate the Medical College of Ohio in Cincinnati. The faculty was in complete control of its operation; no funds were appropriated. The faculty would sell tickets to lectures, which was a common practice throughout the nation.[5]

Turmoil broke out in the third year, and Drake was expelled from the school he had founded. In *Narrative of the Rise and Fall of the Medical College of Ohio* (1822), Drake wrote: "Their motives could not be mistaken. A successful medical school would increase the number of scientific competitors in the city; and raise the standard of excellence in the profession, to a degree with their natural dullness and confirmed indolence in study, would find unattainable."[6]

In 1838, a year before leaving Cincinnati, Drake presented a report to the second convention of the Ohio Medical Society on factors that had combined "to depress the science, dignity and usefulness of the medical profession in the State of Ohio." The report listed eight causes: "1. The study of medicine by illiterates; 2. Students begin to practice before they are qualified; 3. Doctors are so poorly paid that they cannot afford to buy books, etc.; 4. Doctors frequently pay attention to other pursuits besides medicine; 5. Doctors often abandon medicine entirely; 6. Many doctors change their location too frequently; 7. Doctors advertise nostrums of their own; and 8. Doctors do not cultivate social intercourse among each other."[7]

In Otto Juettner's *Daniel Drake and His Followers* (1909), Dr. Samuel Gross described the acrimonious atmosphere at the school. When Gross arrived, Dean Thomas Mitchell told him he could not lecture in the amphitheater. When Gross threatened to withdraw as instructor in anatomy and surgery, he was given his own lecture room in the attic, next to the dissecting room. "I found everything in the department of practical anatomy in the college in the most miserable condition." Gross wrote, "... in short, nothing to denote that any dissections had ever been carried on within its walls." He hired a carpenter and within a week the rooms were ready for classes. Of the eighty-six students in the college, nearly sixty were in Gross's class. He gave three lectures a week on surgical and visceral anatomy, "kept the rooms well supplied with subjects, and thus laid the foundation of the study of practical anatomy, up to that time a nominal matter in the Western States." As was common in Ohio and elsewhere, "resurrectionists" were paid to provide cadavers, and students were discouraged from obtaining their own. Gross is said to have been "the first man in the country to practice systematic dissection and make close examinations of pathological specimens."[8]

Gross left the Medical College of Ohio in 1836 after two years to join Drake at the Cincinnati College Medical Department as the chairman of pathological anatomy, the first program of its kind in the nation. In his autobiography, Gross tells why he left the Medical College of Ohio: "The Faculty was especially a weak one, composed, for the most part, of selfish, narrow-minded men, with moderate scientific attainments, and little ability as teachers. I could not forget the illiberal conduct which had sent me to the garret instead of affording me free access to the amphitheater."[9]

What Mussey knew of conditions at the Medical College of Ohio is not reflected in his writings, although he was acquainted with Drake, a classmate at University of Philadelphia Medical College. Mussey was fifty-six when he left the Bowdoin College faculty in Maine to take the appointment of professor of anatomy at Fairfield in1836. During his first year, it was evident the medical school at Fairfield was declining despite its highly regarded reputation. Competition from new schools in Albany and Geneva as well as Fairfield's financial difficulties led

Mussey to actively seek a position at the Medical College of Ohio. Mussey sent a letter to a former colleague at Dartmouth College, Rev. Calvin Ellis Stowe, asking him to speak with Drake about a position at the Cincinnati school. Drake responded to Mussey with a lengthy letter. The letter disparaged the Medical College of Ohio faculty and offered Mussey a position at his school, the Cincinnati College Medical Department.[10]

Despite Drake's offer and criticism of the Medical College of Ohio, Mussey elected in 1837 to become professor of surgery at Medical College of Ohio, replacing Gross. Mussey remained at the Medical College of Ohio for fourteen years and added to his reputation as a skilled surgeon and scientist. He was considered a leading surgeon in the West with specialties in gynecology and conditions of the eye.[11]

David Prince accompanied Mussey to Cincinnati and graduated in 1839 from the Medical College of Ohio. He then spent a year as an assistant to Mussey. An example of the influence of Mussey on Prince is seen a few years later, when Prince is mentioned as one of the first surgeons in Illinois to successfully perform an ovariotomy.[12] Mussey's influence also became evident later. When Prince opened the first sanitarium in Jacksonville, Illinois, he advertised that the institution specialized in the treatment of eye conditions. One of Prince's two physician sons also became a specialist in treating eyes.

As a student, Prince had an opportunity to witness the significant movement away from the common practice of "heroic medicine": blood-letting and large doses of calomel, a mercury chloride compound that causes vomiting. The belief was this therapy relieved blockages in the system that prevented the body from healing naturally. Initial blood draws were commonly ten ounces. Dr. John Warren wrote in 1813 that, before the 1793 yellow fever outbreak, calomel was prescribed in two-ounce measures; after the outbreak, some physicians administered calomel in doses up to two hundred ounces.[13]

In Cincinnati, this type of therapy was opposed by medical teachers such as Daniel Drake and Medical College of Ohio faculty members Dr. John Eberle, Dr. James Cross, Dean Thomas Mitchell, and Reuben Mussey. They taught rational therapeutic methods and moderation as part of a nationwide reform movement. When Cross moved to the Memphis Medical Institute, it represented itself as "the exponent of reform and progress in medical education, practice and legislation." A society was organized in 1829 in New York by Dr. Wooster Beach to oppose "the abuse of the lancet and the indiscriminate employment of large doses of calomel." When Beach published his 1833 three-volume *American Practice of Medicine,* he was celebrated in Europe, while in America he was called a quack and impostor. Nevertheless, when Beach opened the Reformed Medical College of the City of New York, he attracted many students of medicine, including some from the West.[14]

Benjamin Rush was the primary advocate of heroic medicine. Rush, the only physician to sign the Declaration of Independence, was the leading physician of his time. He also was viewed as a hero because he stayed in Philadelphia when many physicians left at the outbreak in 1793-94 of yellow fever. Rush attributed his success against yellow fever to heroic medicine: multiple doses of calomel and initial "depletion therapy," the drawing of blood three or four times a day. Some patients recovered with only a single draw, he wrote, while others required as much as one hundred ounces of blood to be drawn, depending on the "violence" of the disease.[15]

Rush acknowledged his treatments had critics, but countered that when patients died it was because the therapy was not started soon enough and the patient was not strong enough to fight a severe fever. In *Calomel in America* (2008), Richard M. Swiderski wrote, "Dr. Rush rejoiced in the martial spirit of his conquest of the fever, extended his treatment to all comers. They received the purge as part of a 'depletion therapy' that included bleeding them so copiously that the front yard of Rush's house became sticky with congealed blood and thick with flies."[16]

Calomel originated in India and China in ancient times, although the name was coined in Europe, where it was manufactured in the eighteenth century. Although widely used in the U.S. in the nineteenth century, calomel was unpopular with the American public, so patients often were not told they were being treated with it. It sometimes was administered with a chocolate covering and/or mixed with vegetable emetics. Side effects included gum disease and loosening of teeth. Calomel was used to treat syphilis as well as in therapies for other diseases, especially fevers, and to fight cholera. U.S. Army Surgeon General William A. Hammond prohibited the use of calomel during the Civil War, but it remained in common use as late as the first quarter of the twentieth century.[17]

Reuben Mussey acknowledged the healing power of medicines:

> *Mercury, or quicksilver, has, indeed, a compound adaptedness, for it may be used in the arts as well as in medicine, but this is not true of numberless other things used in the healing art. Senna, rhubarb, Peruvian bark, and numerous other similar things, have no other use than healing, and can be converted to no other purpose. They cannot be placed on the same level, or made to subserve the same ends, as rice, maize, wheat, lentils, for they have properties distinct from them, and they cannot be made to subserve*

the ends which those things are designed to secure. A druggist would starve to death in his shop, though there might be medicines enough there to heal all the diseases in the world. A company of men on a barren island would soon die if there should be nothing else sent to them than a cargo of medicines, they would die if their island produced nothing but quicksilver, rhubarb, and Peruvian bark. The fair conclusion from this fact is, that these things were designed for the purpose of healing; that is, that it was contemplated that there would be diseases demanding a remedy.[18]

However, Mussey went further. He also prescribed a vegetarian diet as part of general therapy and required two days of vegetarian diet before surgery. Mussey had been a vegetarian since 1832, when, at the age of fifty-two, he made the decision to no longer eat animal flesh and eat fish only occasionally. He was convinced to stay a vegetarian when he found, after a few weeks, that he felt stronger and healthier on his new diet.

Mussey prescribed a vegetarian diet for patients facing serious surgery. His students also experimented with the diet, and some found it not only improved their health, but was economical. For instance, two students each spent three months on a diet of wheat meal, milk, potatoes and molasses at a cost of thirty-eight cents a week for each.[19]

Prince was already a vegetarian when he met Mussey. He became a vegetarian at the age of twenty, about the time he entered Fairfield Medical School and a year before Mussey joined the faculty. Prince wrote about being a vegetarian in 1850. His comments were reprinted in a collection of vegetarian literature published in London in 1899, ten years after he died.

> *Though in theory I advocate the use of vegetable food for the world, I myself abstained from animal food, because in addition to theoretic reasons, I find from experience, that this is best for my physical health and mental activity. Now, at the age of 34, I have abstained almost entirely from the use of meat, eggs and fish for 14 years and from tea, coffee and other stimulants for a longer period. My health is uniformly good, my appetite greater that is proper to satiate, my power of resisting heat and cold, and of enduring fatigue, very considerable, and my spirits always cheerful. Occasionally I use cheese, butter, and milk, in small quantity, but so long have I been accustomed to my vegetable diet, that I have only now and then a relish for these, which while the various preparations of meat offer no temptation at all. I passed through the epidemic of cholera, which last year carried off one in ten of our population, and of course attacked a much larger number, without being sick at all, adhering to my usual fare of farinaceous food, vegetables and fruits, and without having a single occasion for opium, or alcohol, in any of their combinations.*[20]

Prince and Mussey were not able to attend the American Vegetarian Convention in New York City in 1850. The convention was the first organized national meeting on vegetarian diets and closed with the formation of the American Vegetarian Society. However, they both wrote letters to the chairman about their absence. Prince wrote: "Animals, as food, will be substituted by the food of vegetable productions, on account of its greater cheapness and abundance, which much of the service now performed by animals will be rendered by steam and galvanism, drawing their force from the immense stores of the vegetation of former years, and from the mines of metals ready to use." Mussey, who was busy with his duties as the recently elected fourth president of the American Medical Association, wrote: "It is delightful to witness the progress the vegetarian principals are making in England; Heaven grant, that in our country a world may soon be commenced, which shall not be arrested until the whole of our vast population shall belong to the train."[21]

One of the chief organizers of the vegetarian convention was Sylvester Graham (1794-1851) of Northampton, Massachusetts. Graham, who invented the graham cracker, was the first diet reformer in America to start a vegetarian movement, Grahamism. Mussey was an ardent Grahamite and aligned himself also with the American Physiological Society as a crusader against the use of alcohol and for vegetarianism.[22]

Among his many writings, Mussey published *Health: Its Friends and Its Foes* in 1862. It is a collection of previous essays and lectures. The book has a common thread of good health to be gained with a vegetarian diet. It devotes most of its attention to diseases associated with tobacco and alcohol consumption as well as numerous case studies about patients' failures, rationalizations, and successes in adoption of healthy eating habits. The text also gives attention to a variety of other topics, including the harmful effects of tight clothing, such as bone-deforming corsets, on women and children, which Mussey attributes to "fashion," as well as to the necessity of ventilation for recovering patients.

There is a religious overtone in the writings of this ardent Christian. "In the great kingdom of living nature man is the only animal that seeks to poison or destroy his own instincts, to turn topsy-turvy the laws of his being, and to make himself as unlike as possible that which he was obviously designed to be," Mussey wrote. And elsewhere:

> *While the myriads of sentient beings spread over the earth adhere with unyielding fidelity to the laws of their several existences, man exerts his superior intellect in attempting to outwit Nature, and to show that she has made an important mistake in his own case. Not satisfied with the symmetry and elegance of form given him by his Creator, he transforms himself into a hideous monster or copies upon his own person the proportions of some disgusting creature far down in the scale of animal being. Not content with loving one thing and loathing another, he perseveres in his attempt to make bitter sweet and sweet bitter, till nothing but the shadow is left of his primitive relishes and aversions.[23]*

Not surprisingly, Mussey also commented on Americans' eating habits. "In the northern section of our country, the annual feasts of Thanksgiving and Christmas, it may be presumed, seldom or never pass without making extra work for the physician, if not for the undertaker. During my professional life I scarcely ever lived through one of these occasions without being consulted for ailments caused by improper eating."[24]

Early in life, Mussey had lost a taste for coffee, tea, and alcohol. (Prince also abstained from tobacco, coffee, tea, and alcohol.) Mussey found alcohol interfered with a sense of wellbeing. Part of the reason, he wrote, was because he inherited a dyspeptic stomach from his father, a country physician in New Hampshire. Dyspepsia was the topic of Mussey's graduate dissertation at Dartmouth Medical College.[25]

It was common practice in this period to give a patient alcohol and morphine before surgery. Mussey believed, from experimentation and observation, that alcohol is poisonous to the human system and that it "positively diminishes the great functions of respiration, capillary, circulation, calorification and meta-morphosis of tissue; and, as a necessary consequence, leads to diminished excretion, and to the accumulation of effete matter, both in the blood and the tissue."[26]

Regarding the medical use of alcohol, Mussey admonished physicians:

> *When alcoholic drinks are employed in cases of prostration or disease, let them be taken under the direction of an intelligent and conscientious physician, who will watch their effects as he would watch those of arsenic or strychnia. The physician who prescribes alcoholic drink for a dyspeptic, to be taken daily for weeks or months, knowing as he does its tendency to generate an uncontrollable appetite for it, takes upon himself a deep responsibility; and if thereby, his patient becomes a confirmed inebriate, he incurs the reflection that he has caused an evil, the amount of which cannot be estimated by any known method of numerical computation.[27]*

Mussey often conducted experiments to find better ways to treat patients who did not respond to known therapies. This practice began when he was a student in Pennsylvania. Mussey questioned Benjamin Rush's contention that substances could not be absorbed through the skin. Mussey conducted an experiment on himself. He submerged himself in a barrel of water containing madder, a red dye. Red dye was expressed in his urine. The experiment received wide attention from physicians and professors, mainly because Mussey had challenged Rush's theory. Several others were able to replicate his results. Rush conducted his own experiments and acknowledged that skin absorption was possible, but he would not fully acknowledge Mussey had proved skin was absorbent. Mussey's graduate dissertation, "Skin Absorption," based on his experiment, was accepted and he received his M.D. degree in 1809.[28]

A widely recorded Mussey surgery involved a patient with reoccurring osteosarcoma, a cancer of the bone. The series of surgeries began with removal of a thumb and forefinger and later the entire arm and shoulder. Subsequently, in an unprecedented procedure, Mussey removed the entire shoulder blade and collar bone. The latter surgery was performed in October 1837. It was the second such operation on record. In 1856, the patient reported to Mussey that he was living and well. Among other recorded surgeries, Mussey performed fifty-two lithotomies (surgical removal of stones from the bladder, kidney, or urinary tract) of which four resulted in deaths.[29]

Mussey was also among the first surgeons to remove ovarian tumors. The first to perform the surgery was Ephraim McDowell of Kentucky, in 1809. An 1852 survey of surgeons in the United States lists Mussey as having performed four ovariotomies with three cures; McDowell is listed as having had seven cases with five cures. David Prince is listed as having performed one ovariotomy, which was successful.[30]

David Prince was thirty-two when he removed the ovarian tumor. It was the first highlight of his career. Prince's passionate approach to surgery reflects the impressions on him made by Mussey, Gross and other teachers. Gross was termed a "zealous anatomist," referring to his emphasis on dissection of cadavers. Prince often practiced dissection in preparation for difficult surgeries, taught dissection to his students and had a remodeled private loft for a dissection theater in the barn behind his home.

Beyond the classroom, these educators had nationwide reputations for their pioneering work and contributions to medical literature. They were interested in establishing professional standards for medicine through medical societies and efforts to persuade legislators to license doctors, putting them above charlatans and quacks. Prince was a charter member of the American Medical Association in 1848, and Mussey was the fourth president of the AMA.

ENDNOTES

[1] Drake, Daniel, M.D. *Narrative of the Rise and Fall of the Medical College of Ohio.* 1822. 17.

[2] "Abolitionism 1830-1850/ The Pro-Slavery Riot in Cincinnati." http://utc.iath.virginia.edu/abolitn/mobhp.html.

[3] Gross. *Autobiography of Samuel D. Gross. M.D.* Philadelphia. George Barrie, Publisher. 1887. 85, 77.

[4] Gross. 70-76.

[5] Juettner, Otto, A.M., M.D. *Daniel Drake and His Followers.* Cincinnati. Harvey Publishing Company. 1909. 190.

[6] Juettner. *Daniel Drakes and His Followers.* 51-52.

[7] Drake. *Narrative of the Rise and Fall of the Medical College of Ohio.* 18.

[8] Juettner. *Daniel Drake and His Followers.* 188.

[9] Juettner. 436.

[10] Gross. *Autobiography.* 63; Jeuttner. *Daniel Drake and His Followers.* 191.

[11] Gross. 64.

[12] Juettner. *Daniel Drake and His Followers.* 165.

[13] Kelly, Howard A. and Burrage, Walter L. *American Medical Biographies.* 943.

[14] Warren, John, M.D. *The Mercurial Practice in Febrile Diseases.* 7.

[15] Juettner, 357.

[16] Rush, Benjamin, M.D. *Medical Inquiries and Observations: containing and account of yellow fever.* 106-109.

[17] Swiderski, Richard M. *Calomel in America: Mercurial Panacea, War, Song and `Ghosts.* Kindle.1398-1400

[18] Swiderski. Kindle. Passim.

[19] Mussey, Reuben D., M.D. *Health: Its Friends and Its Foes.* 1862. 207

[20] Mussey, Reuben D. 220-221.

[21] *Vegetarian Messenger, The.* London. J.M. Burton and Company, steam press. 1852. 95.

[22] Iacobbo, Karen and Michael Iacobbo. *Vegetarian America.* 2004. 71-72. Quoting others.

[23] Iacobbo. passim.

[24] Mussey, Reuben D. *Health: Its Friends and Its Foes.* 92.

[25] Mussey. 196-197.

[26] Mussey. 340-341.

[27] Mussey. 76.

[28] Mussey. 91-92.

[29] Hamilton, John B., M.D., L.L.D. "Life and Times of Doctor Reuben D. Mussey." *Journal of the American Medical Association, Vol. XXVI, No. 14.* April 4, 1896. 651.

[30] Smith, Henry H. *A System of Operative Surgery.* 1852. 35, 785.

III
Rural Medical Practice

"You can succeed if you are in circumstances to live without anxiety and without income for about 3 years, but if you must earn your living for these 3 years the anxiety will either kill you or take the starch of independence out of you. The competition in Springfield is very great and unless a new man can get to the top of a wave, he may be engulfed."

David Prince, M.D. to John
Snyder, M.D. January 31, 1868

Pioneer physicians rarely encountered illness related to poor nutrition. More often, they treated settlers for obstetric problems, fevers, eye diseases, farm accidents, serious fractures, and injuries from Saturday-night fights in the village square.

Immigrant G. W. Barker settled in Waverly, Morgan County. Writing to friends in Connecticut in 1830, he describes the abundance of food: "prairie fowl for the shooting" and "a quarter of fine venison for 2½ cents." Barker chided his friends for warning him he would have trouble finding food in the "wild wilderness." "Sarah is growing quite fleshly," he reported, "has gained flesh since we stopped traveling ... in fact we are all getting fat,"[1]

Illinois immigrants leaving behind the tawny rock-strewn soil of New England found in Illinois a deep black fertile topsoil, where if a stone turned up during plowing, someone put it there. When Dr. Charles Chandler settled east of Beardstown in April 1832, the prairie was described as uncultivated, with undulating vistas, a "Persian rug" colored by tall grasses, wild flowers and scattered groves of cherry, hickory, ash and oak lining meandering streams.[2]

Nevertheless, some New Englanders felt the scenery was not complete. They "greatly missed the golden glow of the dandelion in the grass," according to Dr. Samuel Willard. Willard reported from Carrollton that one settler wrote friends in New England to ask them to bring dandelion seeds when they came – "and thus was it introduced."[3]

After graduating from the Medical College of Ohio in March 1839, David Prince made a brief visit to his family in Payson, Illinois. Prince became reacquainted with his three sisters and now eight-year-old brother Edward. His father operated a dry goods store. Two years later, David Prince Sr. and two other settlers constructed the area's first stone windmill for grinding wheat.

In 1839, David Prince Sr. and his wife joined with eighteen others to form the Congregational Church in Payson. The elder Prince was elected the first deacon of the church. They were assisted by Rev. Asa Turner from Quincy Congregational Church. Rev. Turner was a member of the Yale Band that established Illinois College in Jacksonville in 1829. His younger brother, Jonathan Baldwin Turner, came later to teach at Illinois College.[4]

The first professional public mention of Prince appeared on April 13, 1839, during his family visit. It was an abbreviated advertisement for his practice in the *Quincy Whig,* saying only: "Dr. Prince. Payson." It appears things were improving by the end of 1840 in Quincy when Prince placed a larger advertisement:

> *David Prince, M.D.*
> *Office and residence on Jersey Street, South side, between Third and Fourth.*
> *N.B. Particular attention is paid to affections (sic) of the Eyes and to deformities.*
> Quincy Whig, *December 25, 1840.*

In addition to his struggles to establish a practice, Prince had personal matters with which to deal, both pleasant and unpleasant. In 1841, Prince returned to Cincinnati to marry Mary Jane Dawson, a schoolteacher. They had three children and adopted a niece of his wife. All four of the children died young, and Mary Jane herself died during a cholera epidemic St. Louis in 1849.[5]

Prince advertised in a Jacksonville newspaper, sixty-six miles east of Payson. He anticipated he would be there for sixteen weeks beginning in late 1843 when he was recruited to teach at the Illinois College Medical Department.

> *DAVID PRINCE, Jr. M.D.*
> *At Payson, Adams Co. Ill. 15 miles southeast of Quincy, of which place he was recently a resident, devotes particular attention to the surgical part of his profession, and especially to diseases of the eye and to deformities of the feet and other parts. It should be generally known that*

Club or crooked feet admit in most cases of being restored to the natural form, and Strabismus or cross eye generally admits to cure.
    Illinois Statesman, J. B. Turner, editor. April 29, 1843.

Prince found it difficult to establish himself as a physician and surgeon. His arrival in Illinois closely followed a chaotic financial period throughout the state. After the Blackhawk War in 1832, increased westward migration and speculation drove up land prices. By 1837, an economic panic spread from the East, creating lean times, bank failures, and a general lack of available cash. This greatly affected how doctors were paid, if at all.

Country doctors often made house calls up to ten miles away, surgeons up to fifteen miles away. Startup costs included a bridle horse – a good one would be able to trot evenly, to avoid breaking bottles of medicine in the saddlebag, yet be strong enough to ford a stream when necessary – plus a saddle, medicine bag as well as food and shelter for the horse. However, a saddle bag wasn't convenient when working at the side of a patient. A doctor who could afford a horse and buggy found traveling somewhat easier and could use a more convenient box with compartments for medicine bottles. But whatever form of transportation used, traveling physicians had to contend with rudimentary roads – little more than paths – that were dusty when dry or muddy after spring rains.[6]

Prince kept detailed records of his charges. His surgery account books for 1845 to 1847 show a total income of six hundred and forty dollars. Other income came from his general practice and from student tickets for classes at the Illinois College Medical Department where he taught from November to March.[7]

Patient fees were not always paid by patients. Some were paid by others or by notes. Prince recorded payments from a probate court, from Illinois College for attending President Julian M. Sturtevant, from an estate and from a referring physician. There is a much longer list of articles taken in lieu of cash, such as: "paid by my blacksmith bill," a saddle pad, squashes, butter, a load of hay, pasturing a cow and twenty bushels of corn. Two accounts are listed as forgiven with one noted as "gone to Iowa for good."[8]

Collecting fees was an ongoing problem, as seen in a January 8, 1868 letter he wrote to Dr. John Snyder of Virginia concerning a patient Snyder referred to Prince: "As to Martin, I have no idea he has a sober thought of ever paying my bill. If you could get it collected without compromising yourself. I should be thankful for your services but I do not think you had better be connected with the progress except as an interest. I think you had better give me the name of a good collector and I will send him the bill anew so that it will not seem that you have had anything to do with it."[9]

Prince's surgery fees included: "Fracture of femur, child $9; Removing placenta $5; Circumcision $5; Obstetric attendance $5; Obstetric attendance $20; Amputating tonsils $1; Removing splinter from hand $1; Applying splint to finger $1; Injury to hip $10; Amputating thigh $50; Use of Electro-magnetic machine $6; and Fracture of Tibia, ten months old $30."[10]

Nineteenth-century physicians struggled financially in the East as well as the pioneer West. Eastern physicians were often active in more than one profession, serving also as judges or preachers. The lifestyle carried over to the West. One physician in Aurora, Illinois told a friend that "one day he visited his patients, tried a law suit and preached a funeral service." Perhaps more consistent with their work, some doctors opened drug stores next to their offices. Competition from the growing numbers of physicians in the East, due in great part to the proliferation of medical schools, led many to move west.[11]

The fertile prairie was also an attraction. Medical historian George H. Weaver comments: "Anterior to 1840, nine tenths of all the physicians who had located themselves in this region, had done so with reference to pursuing agriculture and the avowed intention of abandoning medical practice; most of whom either from necessity of the case, or from finding more truth than poetry in pounding out rails, resumed their profession, and divided their attention between farming and medicine."[12]

A Prince contemporary who struggled in central Illinois was John T. Hodgen (1826-1882). Hodgen grew up in Pittsfield, Illinois, graduating in 1848 from the University of Missouri Medical Department. After graduation, Hodgen spent a year as resident physician at St. Louis City Hospital, then joined the faculty of Missouri Medical College. He held several positions in anatomy and physiology there from 1849 to 1862. Between terms, Hodgen worked at establishing a private practice. He returned to Pittsfield in 1849, but found prior residency was not helpful. He gave up after two years and left for California to join the Gold Rush. Hodgen returned soon, with no gold. He went back to St. Louis, broke, to try once again to establish a private practice, but at the end of the medical school term in February 1850 he returned again to private practice in Pittsfield.[13]

In May of 1854, Hodgen wrote a plaintive letter to Dr. John Snyder, his colleague in Cass County. He complained about the lack of work and asked the rhetorical question: "Do you find anyone who doesn't think more of some old quack than of yourself?" Later, Hodgen mentions the possibility of starvation because of competition from "thousands of Eclectics,

Hydropathists, Rooters, and Steamers who are meteorically illuminating the world."[14] When Hodgen again returned to St. Louis, he had the same problem establishing a private practice, until an incident turned around his fortunes. He was walking in a park one day when he was attracted to crowd at the edge of the lake. A Black man was drowning in the lake. Hodgen immediately went in to save the man. He brought the man ashore and proceeded to give him mouth-to-mouth resuscitation. The man was revived, much to the excitement of the crowd. Word of the incident spread through St. Louis, and soon after Hodgen had more patients than he could handle.[15]

Competition for patients was keen among doctors, and trained physicians were price competitive among themselves. But not all doctors had preparation beyond a year or two with a trained doctor as a preceptor; some practiced without training or a diploma. This led to some jealousy of those trained in eastern schools when they began to flood the West beginning in the 1830s.

Frauds – traveling salesmen peddling patent medicines, quacks, herb doctors, steam doctors, dentists, bleeders and bonesetters with no knowledge of anatomy – were even more of a problem.[16] Homeopathy (a medical system based on the idea that the body can heal itself), was growing in popularity when Prince began his practice. Many trained physicians, including Prince, referred to themselves as "allopathic" practitioners to distinguish themselves from those offering alternative medicine.

Midwives, not physicians, attended many births. Some midwives called in doctors when they recognized a problem developing. Others waited until the mother was greatly distressed before they sought a doctor's help. Jacksonville's first midwife, Katherine Kendall Carson, delivered more than three thousand babies. She learned medicine from her physician father and assisted him with patient care. He taught her "lessons of cleanliness and careful record keeping."[17]

Patient relations were sometimes strained by religion. In one instance, a minister came to a physician's home office to report on his sick wife. The minister noticed a blackboard on which the doctor had written sentences in Latin and Greek for his two sons to translate. The minister pronounced the work profane and suggested it would be better to write verses from the New Testament.

They argued vehemently at length about diseases supposedly caused by devil-possession. The doctor argued: "Many diseases have, indeed, been demonstrated to be due to other causes, not a single disease that has even been investigated carefully has been found to have been produced by devil-possession. Why do you have your wife take my medicine? Why don't you exorcise the devil instead?"

The minister set down the bottle of medicine, turned and walked out the door. The doctor was left in agony, for the minister was one of his best friends, a good companion with whom he had discussed Latin and Greek translations. Then suddenly, the minister returned. He picked up the bottle of medicine, explaining: "My wife is very much addicted to human medicine. We shall have to make concessions in her case. It is absolutely necessary to do this." The doctor was much relieved.[18]

Religion was a personal issue for some physicians. Pioneer physician Andrew Wilson Elder was conflicted about following his moral duty to patients and his religious obligation to honor the Sabbath. Elder came from Lexington, where he graduated from Transylvania University Medical College in 1823. The next year, his parents moved to Morgan County, Elder joined them, becoming the only physician between Jacksonville and Springfield, about thirty miles apart.

Elder was a pious and active member of the Church of Christ, but his patients sometimes became sick or children were born on Sundays. His conscience bothered him. Elder felt he could resolve the conflict by taking calls on Sunday without charging for them. It turned out his calls for treatments during the week dropped off fifty percent, and he became so busy on Sundays that he couldn't attend church services. While this soothed his conscience somewhat, it also decreased his income.

Not able to sustain this plan, which also was wearing him out physically, Elder changed his policy. He decided to see patients in his home on Sundays, free of charge. As a result, every Sunday, his house became crowded with the sick and maimed, and they brought family members with them. "It converted his house, every Sunday, not only into a free-hospital, but a tavern also, enslaving his wife and family, consuming his medicines, and exhausting his larder," according to Carl Black in *Medical Practice in Illinois Before Hard Roads*. Elder soon gave up the reforms and returned to his old practice.[19]

One of the main difficulties for doctors was that things did not always go smoothly with patients. Many patients had personal preferences for therapies, such as self-medication or family favorite nostrums. Other patients didn't follow their physicians' orders for administering medicine or limiting activity. Some patients turned to suing their physician when unhappy with the results of the physician's treatment or surgery, while others refused to pay the physician's fee.

Medical historian Otto Juettner, writing in 1909 about Western medicine in the nineteenth century, offers the following description of the physician's dilemma: "The doctor is an angel of mercy when he appears at the bedside of his patient, ready and anxious to relieve suffering and dispute every inch of ground in the battle with death. After the patient has recovered, the doctor, with bill in hand for services rendered, is quickly metamorphosed into a demon incarnate. Patients, who owe health and life to the skill and loyalty of the physician, seem to suffer from a sudden loss of memory. All obligations, all debts of gratitude are forgotten."[20]

Some examples of how physicians collected fees are illustrated in two advertisements appearing in Jacksonville's *Western Observer* in 1830.

> *NOTICE*
> *All persons indebted to the estate of the late Dr. Benjamin P. Miller, are requested to settle the same immediately, by note or otherwise. William Miller, Ex'r*

> *THE LAST WAY*
> *All persons indebted to Dr. Ero Chandler are expected to call and settle their accounts, by note or payment, between this and the 25th of December; otherwise they will find them in the hands of the Justice of the Peace in Jacksonville, as I have not time to make personal collections. E. Chandler. Nov . 20, 1830*

Dr. Ero Chandler was, indeed, a busy man. His financial success runs counter to that of many other contemporary doctors. In the same year the above advertisement appeared, he was a subscriber to Illinois College; donated a building lot for the Presbyterian Church; and donated other property for the Jacksonville Female Academy, the first school for women west of Ohio. As a farsighted citizen, he laid out a large subdivision, Chandler's Addition, on the west side of Jacksonville.

Chandler was born in Vermont and educated in Ohio. His father was a physician and a descendant of the Pilgrim leader Miles Standish. At twenty-five, he settled in 1821as the first doctor in Jacksonville. He arrived with only the clothes he was wearing and riding a "broken down horse." He charged seventy-five cents to visit a patient if he could do so on foot and the visit didn't take all day; it was one dollar if he had to rent a horse. Eventually, he accumulated land, which sold for $1.25 per acre, and spent much of his time on his farm, raising crops and livestock. He practiced in Jacksonville until 1836, when he moved to Hancock County, where he lived until his death in 1883.[21]

The following anecdotes are from *My Second Life* (1944), the autobiography of Dr. Thomas Hall Shastid. Shastid was a diarist, a habit he learned from his physician father, as well as a highly regarded ophthalmologist and medical historian. Shastid's 1,159-page autobiography includes his experiences as a youth in Pittsfield, Illinois, when he traveled with his father as he visited patients in Pike County.[22]

In 1884, when Shastid was eighteen, his father agreed he should spend a summer as a medical apprentice with Prince at the David Prince Sanitarium. Shastid's first participation in an operation involved an ovariectomy during which he was assigned to pump what was referred to as "Lister's Donkey Engine." As the "donkey," the surgeon's apprentice worked the handle of the engine on a tripod, spraying a cloud of weak carbolic acid solution "to kill principally, the micro-organisms in the atmosphere."[23]

Shastid once visited a fellow physician he refers to as Dr. Misanthropus. The doctor asked him to come to his office to examine his eyes. Shastid describes the doctor as "hard-boiled." Upon examining the doctor's eyes, Shastid found "a truly terrible sight, snow-blank retinitis and indubitable evidence of chronic inflammation of the kidneys." As they discussed the condition, a patient, Mr. Franklin, came in, insisting on seeing the doctor.

Shastid was told "This man is a curious fellow, a fault finder with all his doctors, I hear – keep your seat." Shastid relates the conversation he witnessed between "Dr. Misanthropus" and the patient:

> *In came the man, took the easiest chair for himself without any invitation, and then, before the least sidetracking of his thought could occur, poured out a long harsh tale about the ignorance, double-dealing, and absolutely inexcusable mistakes of all the other doctors he had formerly consulted. "In fact," concluded the man, "The whole medical profession is nothing but arrant humbug and the very vilest fraud. Now, if you can't do anything for me, I want you honestly to say so – but no more quackery will I tolerate."*

> *I thought all at once of the old, so commonly used, expression in the backwoods country, "Them's fightin words in these hyer parts, stranger."*

But when Franklin had finished his tirade, Doctor Misanthropus bespoke him as gently as any "suckling dove." Said he, in conclusion, "And I do think know something that will be very good for you."

You do? For me?"

"Yes, sir, indeed I do. Something that will help you greatly."

"And what is that, may I ask?"

"Egress," responded Misanthropus. "The fluid of egress."

"Never heard of it before," commented Franklin.

"Come this way," instructed the doctor. And, having been followed curiously by the patient to the back door, the doctor suddenly threw the door open and the man out.

The doctor, having washed his hands meticulously, asked me to prescribe for him, Misanthropus. That I did and departed.[24]

All the problems described above were a great concern to physicians in Illinois who had diplomas. A small group arranged an informal meeting in Springfield on June 9, 1840 to organize the Medical Society of Illinois, electing Dr. John Todd as president. (Prince did not attend this meeting, although he attended subsequent meetings). Six of the twelve attendees were from Sangamon County. Others were from as far away as Chicago and Joliet. Among the medical schools represented were Harvard University Medical Department, University of Pennsylvania, Jefferson Medical College and Maryland Medical College; two of those in attendance were graduates of Fairfield Medical College, New York.[25]

The physicians and surgeons attending the meeting agreed to address an open letter to the medical profession of Illinois. The letter was published June 19, 1840 in Springfield's *Illinois State Journal* with a request that all Illinois newspapers publish the letter once or more. A portion of the article included the following:

> *Hitherto we have been like a vessel cast upon a boisterous ocean, without compass or helm; we have acted solitary and alone, without harmony or concert; but when we see hundreds of our fellow-citizens and worthy friends annually sacrificed by the empirical prescriptions of charlatan professors, on the altars of ignorance erected with the very temple of Aesculapius by rude and unskillful hands, is it not time for us to act? We think so, but not by declaring war against mountebanks and uneducated pretenders to the art of healing within our boarders, but by digesting a plan that shall be calculated in its legitimate operations to benefit the people, instruct the unlearned, inform ourselves and elevate the entire profession above all mercenary considerations to a station of superior mental, moral and medical excellence.*[26]

The group adjourned with an agreement to meet again in December 1840, hopefully with one or more physicians from each county. Getting sufficient regular attendance was difficult; many meetings were canceled. On December 16, 1847, the society met in Springfield and re-elected Todd as president. Prince, then living in Payson, was elected secretary. In addition, Prince was elected a delegate to the National Medical Convention. A report on medical education was given by Dr. Edward Mead of the Illinois College Medical Department.

The 1847 meeting was followed by fewer meetings, as well as less correspondence, and some physicians stopped attending meetings, according to records kept by Todd. Among those who were active during this period were Drs. Prince, Charles Hughs of Rochester and Moses Knapp of Logan County.

The Medical Society of Illinois was superseded by the Illinois State Medical Society in 1850, when members approved a state charter and a new constitution.[27]

ENDNOTES

[1] Crellin, John N. *Medical Care in Pioneer Illinois*. 11. Citing note 19 of G. W. Barker papers (18Nov1830 Manuscripts Illinois State Historical Library)

[2] Chandler, Josephine Craven. "Dr. Charles Chandler His place in the American Scene." *Journal of the Illinois State Historical Society* (1908-1984), Vol. 24, No. 3 (Oct., 1931). 369-552. 420.

[3] Willard, Samuel. "Personal Reminiscences of Life in Illinois – 1830 to 1850." *Transactions of the Illinois State Historical Society* 11 (1906): 73-87. 1906

[4] *Quincy and Adams County History*. "History of Payson and Plainville, Il." Supervising Editor Judge Lyman McCarl. The Lewis Publishing Company, Chicago and New York. 1919.

[5] Shastid, Thomas Hall. *My Second Life*. 568.

[6] Black, Carl E., M.D." *Medical Practice in Illinois Before Hard Roads*." 16-18. Black describes travel for pioneer physicians as: "This era in medicine in central Illinois may be roughly divided into days of (1) horseback and bridle paths, (2) horse and buggy, (3) automobile, (4) dirt road, and (5) hard road."

[7] Black. papers Box 15. Abraham Lincoln Presidential Library, Springfield, Illinois.

[8] Black. copied from Prince's diary. Black Papers Box 5. Abraham Lincoln Presidential Library,

[9] David Prince to John Snyder. January 8, 1868. Snyder Papers. Box 4. Abraham Lincoln Presidential Library. Springfield, IL.

[10] Black. copied from Prince's diary. Black Papers. Box 5. Abraham Lincoln Presidential Library.

[11] Weaver, George Howlett. *Beginnings of Medical Education in and near Chicago / The institutions and the men*. 5.

[12] Weaver, George Howlett. 6.

[13] Shastid. 70.

[14] Crellin, John N. *Medical Care in Pioneer Illinois*. 46.

[15] Shastid. 160-161.

[16] Shastid. 438.

[17] Barwick, Gary Jack and Kay, Betty Carlson. *Images of America JACKSONVILLE ILLINOIS The Traditions Continue.* 12; *History of Morgan County: Its Past and Present.* Donnelly, Lloyd & Company. 336-337. http://morgan.illnoisgenweb.org/1878/index.html.

[18] Shastid. 324-326.

[19] Black, Carl E. "Medical Practice in Illinois Before Hard Roads." 6-7.

[20] Juettner, Otto, A.M., M.D. *Daniel Drake and His Followers.* Cincinnati. Harvey Publishing Company. 1909. 22.

[21] Bateman, Newton; Selby, Paul and Currey, J. Seymour. *Historical Encyclopedia of Illinois.* 841-842; "Dr. Ero Chandler", *Jacksonville Daily Journal*, March 30, 1917; Eames, Charles M. *Historic Morgan and Classic Jacksonville.* Jacksonville, 34-35.

[22] Shastid. 356-357.

[23] Shastid. 566.

[24] Shastid. 38-39

[25] Zeuch, Lucius H., M.D. *History of Medical Practice in Illinois. Vol. I Preceding 1850.* 394-395

[26] Zeuch. 394.

[27] Zeuch. 396.

IV
Illinois College Medical Department

"The medical school at Jacksonville, though short lived (1843-1848), left a deep impress on the medical history of Illinois."

Otto F. Kampmeier, M.D., *"Medical Libraries in Illinois Preceding 1900"*

David Prince was always interested in teaching, and he often proctored students preparing for medical school. His first opportunity to gratify that desire in a formal setting came in 1843, when Illinois College opened a medical department and recruited him to be chairman of anatomy and surgery. Unfortunately, he was almost immediately accused of grave robbing – specifically, exhuming the body of a former Illinois governor – to provide students with a cadaver for dissection.

Illinois College had had an optimistic beginning when it was organized in 1829. Rev. John M. Ellis, a Presbyterian missionary from New Hampshire, sought to establish a "seminary of learning" in Illinois. Ellis led a site search committee under the auspices of the St. Louis-based Presbytery of Missouri and Illinois.

Ellis' committee chose Jacksonville, Illinois, but the Presbytery of Missouri rejected the choice as being on the wrong side of the Mississippi River. In response, Ellis and others formed an independent board of trustees. With strong local support, the trustees were able to solicit subscriptions in cash, materials, and labor. They bought land and had a two-story brick building constructed.[1]

The first attempt to get a state charter for the college in 1829 was rejected by legislators who had emigrated from southern states and considered it a "Yankee enterprise." A second effort for a charter was introduced in 1835 along with charters for three other proposed colleges. This time, with the additional backing of Governor Joseph Duncan of Jacksonville, the Jacksonville school received its charter. Later in 1835, Illinois College became the first institution in Illinois to graduate a collegiate class. The two graduates were Richard Yates, who became governor during the Civil War, and Jonathan E. Spillman, who became a minister.[2]

An article Ellis wrote about plans for the college in a denomination newspaper inspired divinity students at Yale Theological Seminary. Seven students contacted Ellis, accepted the challenge and left for Illinois after they were ordained as Congregational ministers. The group became known as the "Yale Band." Most of the members were named trustees of the college. In addition, the Congregational missionaries would preach in Presbyterian churches and recruit promising students.[3] The first two members of the Yale Band to go to Illinois were Julian Sturtevant and Theron Baldwin; Sturtevant taught at Illinois College and Baldwin went to Vandalia, then the state capital, to minister to the Presbyterian church and conduct missionary work.

In Illinois College's earliest years, trustees considered establishing departments of law, medicine and theology. The school faced competition for both students and endowment funds, especially after Knox College opened in Galesburg, one hundred miles north of Jacksonville, in 1837. Endowments for the proposed law and theology departments were not forthcoming, but if the college was to survive, trustees believed they had to create a medical school.

However, Illinois College was deep in debt when the medical department opened in 1843. Until 1837, when a nationwide economic panic swept into Illinois, the college had successfully raised funds by selling building lots surrounding the eighty-acre campus. The Panic of 1837, however, left the college with one hundred thousand dollars in unpaid subscriptions and property taxes due.

"Most of the subscriptions proved utterly worthless," Julian Sturtevant, the college's first teacher and president from 1845 to 1876, wrote in his autobiography. "Little either of principal or interest was ever paid."[4]

"Unoccupied town lots, and to a considerable extent unimproved lands, were not property in its true sense. They produced nothing but taxes," Sturtevant wrote, adding that the decade following the 1837 panic was "the darkest period in the history of Illinois College." Donations dried up, and professors suffered from the financial shortfall as total salaries were reduced from one hundred thousand dollars in 1839, to seven hundred dollars in 1842, and to six hundred dollars in 1843; even then, they were often in arrears.[5]

To make the new medical department feasible, the trustees organized the department as financially independent of the literary school. The medical instructors would lease space in the Chapel "as the academical faculty shall think can be spared from the purposes of the academical department." Furthermore, the four medical professors would collect fees directly from students for the sixteen weeks of lectures. A full course of lectures for a student was sixty dollars; private dissection tickets were five dollars more. Students interested in missionary careers were permitted to attend medical lectures for free, not including dissections. The new department also conducted a free dispensary for local residents on Mondays and Tuesdays. Led by Prince and Dr. Daniel Stahl, professor of theory and practice, it was intended to give students practical instruction, including use of the stethoscope and other matters of importance.[6]

The first medical school catalog described "a respectable medical library belonging to the institution and embracing the best modern work upon the various branches of medicine. Students have access to teachers' private libraries that include texts in French, German and English."[7]

Four departments made up the medical curriculum. Prince taught anatomy and surgery, Stahl covered theory and practice of medicine, Samuel Adams taught chemistry and materia medica, and Henry Jones instructed students on obstetrics and diseases of women. A "Board of Censors," made up of area physicians and faculty, examined the graduates before conferring M.D. degrees. Fourteen students attended a sixteen-week course of lectures in the first year, with five of those students graduating in 1845. The number of medical students varied from year to year, as some would leave after a single year.

However, Illinois College quickly had more medical students attending classes than were enrolled in the literary college. Medical students attended over a shorter period and paid the largest fees. In 1913, Carl Black wrote an article for the Illinois Medical Journal: "In 1845, there were thirty students in the medical department and only twenty-seven in the college proper. There were twelve irregular students and twenty in the preparatory department, making a total of eighty-nine students in the institution. During the 1845-1846 school year, twenty-eight medical students took private dissecting tickets."[8]

According to Prince's account books, reviewed by Black, his biographer, Prince not only advanced money to students for board, books and clothing, he provided them with dissection material on credit. The account books show also that students repaid most of this money in the years after, often with interest.

Samuel Willard of Carrollton graduated from Illinois College in 1843 and was one of the last graduates of the medical department in 1848. He said of Prince: "Dr. Prince was not a fluent lecturer; he seemed to struggle with the dialect of technical terms which he insisted upon using; perhaps if he had had the collegiate education in Greek and Latin he would have spoken more easily. He was not without his anecdotes and humor."[9]

The literary faculty watched the medical department take shape with some concern, especially, according to Black, about dissections. Some of the literary faculty "felt a repugnance for the men of the dissecting room," Black wrote.[10]

Controversy over dissection broke out at Illinois College within three months of the start of medical classes. In January 1844, Prince and his fourteen medical students were accused of exhuming for dissecting the body of former Governor Duncan, who died on January 15, 1844, and was buried at Diamond Grove Cemetery a half-mile south of the campus.

Angry residents of Jacksonville stormed onto the college campus in protest. The mob, determined to tar and feather Prince, surrounded the Chapel (now Beecher Hall), where anatomy classes were held. It is not clear exactly what happened next. The

Jacksonville Daily Journal office burned in 1859, destroying all previous editions, and no other first-person accounts of the incident have been found. However, medical historian George H. Weaver wrote in 1925: "Only the timely presence of Dr. Samuel Adams, with assurance and promise to the family and public, prevented a catastrophe." Adams, professor of chemistry, was the leader in the medical department and had helped recruit the faculty. Adams also was well known to the Jacksonville community. He had practiced locally for several years before the medical department opened in 1843 and was one of several consultants during Duncan's two-week-illness prior to his death.[11]

Some historians claim the closure of the medical department in 1848 was caused by the "anatomy question" and community opposition. Sappol's *A Traffic of Dead Bodies* (2002) includes Illinois College in a table listing "Crowd actions against American Medical Schools 1765-1884." The list included: "1848 Jacksonville, IL. Rioters force a local medical school to close, due to a lack of cadavers." Sappol found seventeen anatomy riots in several states over the period.[12]

This issue is addressed in a 1966 biography of David Prince by Jacksonville physician Dr. Frank E. Norbury: "Duncan, sixth Governor of Illinois, died in Jacksonville on January 15, 1844. Illinois College Medical School had only been in existence two and one-half months and was still holding classes in Beecher Hall which had no real dissecting room. Although Duncan's body might have been dissected in a barn or elsewhere, the Medical School continued for more than four years after his death. Therefore, the dissection of Duncan, if it ever occurred at all, was certainly not responsible for the closing of the school." (It also seems unlikely that any dissections were performed in the Chapel, since the literary faculty controlled what space the medical faculty could use. Without refrigeration, the literary faculty would not have tolerated decomposing corpses in the Chapel.)[13]

Issues regarding the medical department's use of Chapel space were resolved after the first year of classes. In July 1844, a two-story frame workshop building sitting idle at the corner of Mound Avenue and Lincoln Street was remodeled to accommodate the medical department. It had a laboratory and dissecting room on the first floor and a large lecture room on the second with a small office for professors.[14]

In the first year, the medical department's anatomy classes have been described as essentially didactic with supporting materials such as skeletons, anatomy charts and a library. However, Prince always contended that dissection material for his anatomy classes was essential and that the bodies were not locally sourced. The first catalogue of the Illinois College Medical Department likewise specified that "anatomy material comes from abroad."

In a 1907 article, "A Pioneer Medical School," Black opined that the Jacksonville community and the faculty of other departments were always suspicious that Prince and his students robbed graves for dissection material. A footnote in a 1913 reprint of the article added that an early student at the medical department took issue with Black's comments. The student reported: "This does not agree entirely with what you said before about raids on graveyards. But every corpse for dissection was taken from a barrel, sure dripping with alcohol. What I may happen to know about how some bodies got there is neither printed nor written."[15]

The demand for dissection material in America, especially for rural schools, was so great that transportation of cadavers became a common practice. The Illinois dissection law in force in 1844 had been enacted in 1825 and amended in 1833. The law provided it was unlawful to disinter the dead for the purpose of dissection "or any surgical or anatomical experiment or any other purpose." The penalty for anyone convicted of violating the law was a fine not to exceed five hundred dollars and imprisonment in jail "not more than twelve and not less than three months." The law was made more definite in 1833, when the code regarding murder provided that the punishment for murder would be hanging and that "the court may order, on the application of any respectable surgeon or surgeons which the body of the convict shall, after death be delivered to such surgeon or surgeons for dissection."[16]

In 1841, George Gardner was tried in Morgan County Circuit Court for murder and found guilty. He was sentenced by Judge Stephen A. Douglas to be hung and his body made available for dissection. However, Gardner escaped from the Morgan County jail before the execution date.[17]

Shipping cadavers from abroad may have been impossible in frontier communities, but Jacksonville had an advantage. In 1839, the Northern Cross Railroad completed laying track from Meredosia, on the Illinois River, to Jacksonville twenty-three miles east. It was the first railroad in Illinois. Builders planned to extend the line to Springfield the following year.

It is likely that dissection material reached Jacksonville in barrels delivered to one or another of the city's sixteen hardware stores. The barrels would be labeled perhaps as alcohol and marked that they would be picked up by someone from the medical school.

Many improvements to the medical school were announced in the 1845 catalogue, which included a review of the new features. Among the items were cabinets of anatomical preparations and materia medica, Bougery and Jacob color plates, Jean Cruveilhier's *Pathological Anatomy* with colored engravings of European import, apparatus, and plates for illustrating practical obstetrics and surgical operations performed before a class.[18]

The Medical Library

Five titles of the once extensive Illinois College Medical Department library have been returned to the campus. These five volumes of the peripatetic library were returned in September 2013, 165 years after the closing of the medical department. One of the five books, the oldest in the group, is a Latin anatomy text published in 1703 in Germany.

The transfer included an additional sixty-six books that were a part of the Morgan County Medical Society library. Prince is the common thread in this story.

The description of the Illinois College medical library that appeared in the school's first catalogue was reprinted in the *History of Medical Practice in Illinois, 1850-1900* (1955). In the section "Medical Libraries in Illinois Before 1900," medical historian Otto Kampmeier described the library as containing "many very old books, valuable historically and as book rarities, a number of them in Latin." As for its disposition, Kampmeier wrote:

> *With the closing of the doors of the medical department of Illinois College in 1848, the fate of its library, for the growth of which much money*

and energy had been spent, assumed an increased interest. Contrary to what usually happens to a virtually abandoned collection of that kind, the course of this one is fairly clear. For almost half a century it remained stored away dusty and useless in the old library in Beecher Hall. The library remained stored in Beecher Hall for forty-six years until it was turned over in trust to the Morgan County Medical Society in 1894 "to make it serviceable for physicians and students."[19]

The Morgan County Medical Society began formal meetings in 1866. At a meeting in the YMCA in 1888, prior to the transfer from Illinois College, the members appropriated $100 to buy books to start a library. Soon after, David Prince came in with several books, put them in an empty bookcase, and declared: "This is the beginning of the Library of the Morgan County Medical Society."

Many donations and bequests followed. The sons of David Prince, after his passing, donated his entire library. Dr. T. J. Pitner donated a large portion of his private library. In 1898, Abbe Pierson, the granddaughter of Dr. Daniel Pierson of Augusta, Illinois, donated his library. In 1899, Dr. N. S. Read of Chandlerville bequeathed his library to the society and in 1901 the widow of Dr. A. H. Kellogg donated "about one hundred and fifty volumes." A donation was also made by Frank P. Norbury of Jacksonville. Greene Vardiman Black donated a first-printing copy of his internationally celebrated two-volume *Operative Dentistry* (1908).[20]

Under an agreement in 1903 with the Jacksonville Public Library, the society moved its library to the new Carnegie building of the Jacksonville Public Library and arranged to hold its meetings there as well. Carl Black, the son of Greene Vardiman Black, was the society's librarian. He reported at the end of 1905 the society's library held 1,789 books (319 duplicates from gift collections) that had been "properly accessioned, catalogued, plated, labeled, and shelved."[21]

By 1940, both the medical society collection and the Jacksonville Public Library collection took up so much shelf space that public library asked the medical society to remove its collection. The medical society boxed up the books and took them to Passavant Hospital. The hospital did not have a librarian, but did offer space for storage.

Carl Black, a Fellow of the Chicago-based American College of Surgeons in 1940, initiated correspondence with the ACS archivist, Margueriete Prime, inviting her to visit Jacksonville to review the collection of books, biographies and monographs. They reached an agreement to transfer the library to ACS. Black wrote to ACS director Dr. Bowman C. Crowell May 10, 1941 reporting that the society had voted to donate the library and it would be delivered by truck ten days later. Four thousand volumes were delivered.[22]

Prime submitted an announcement of the acquisition to ACS members, listing many of the authors. She wrote: "Possibly the most interesting item in the entire group is comprised of the handwritten 'Notes on Surgery from the Lectures of Dr. Physick, Professor of Surgery in the University of Pennsylvania, 1812-1813' by Daniel Pierson." Physick, one of the foremost surgeons of his time, is often referred to as the father of American surgery. He had among his patients the U. S. Supreme Court's first chief justice, John Marshall, President Andrew Jackson, and Dolly

Madison. This notebook is among the titles that have been returned to Illinois College.[23]

In recent years, many items from the ACS collections have been distributed to university medical libraries, according to ACS archivist, Susan Rishworth. In 2011, a project was started to create a database of the ACS remaining historical and rare books. When the database was completed, this author, acting on behalf of Illinois College, asked the ACS to separate books with faceplates identifying the original owners as the Morgan County Medical Society or Illinois College. Seventy-one books were identified as such and transferred to the Schewe Library at Illinois College. Authors of some of these books are easily recognized, such as Lavoisier, Joseph Lister, Daniel Drake and Benjamin Rush.[24] (See Appendix A for a complete list of the seventy-one titles.)

These seventy-one books are a very small portion of the four thousand books donated to the ACS by the Morgan County Medical Society in 1941. Nevertheless, they give a glimpse into the past and allow a view of the studiousness of nineteenth century physicians in Morgan County as well as the wide range of medical literature available to them.

Illinois College Medical Department closes

Illinois College's financial plight led to a variety of alternative ideas. Julian Sturtevant and Theron Baldwin, members of the Yale Band, corresponded regularly. On March 30, 1847, Sturtevant, by then the second president of Illinois College, wrote a lengthy letter to trustee Baldwin. The letter was a long discussion of financial conditions and alternatives.

Sturtevant wrote that "some" were discussing a political solution to the college's problem, in particular Morgan County state representatives William Thomas and Cyrus Edwards. "There are men among the leading democratic politicians of this state who have formed the design of making this college the State University," Sturtevant wrote, although he opposed the idea as a "monstrous folly." He saw the design not as a matter of whether it will or will not be college "but whether it shall be controlled by the principles of Protestant Christianity or not."[25]

In 1846, the trustees again approved a plan to sell lands not used for instruction. If that failed, Sturtevant believed the only choice would be to "suspend instruction and sell the buildings." Ultimately, however, the sale raised thirty thousand dollars. "By the spring of 1847, most of the salaries due the faculty were paid. For the first time in years Sturtevant was free from anxiety and he could now spend fifty cents without apprehension," according to sixth president Charles Rammelkamp in a centennial publication.[26]

The Trustees proposed to construct a new Medical Hall under the existing terms of keeping the medical department financially separate from the literary school. Subsidizing the medical school would have become more onerous for the medical faculty after the 1847-1848 classes.

Sturtevant to Baldwin, March 30, 1847: "A movement is now in progress to erect a Medical Hall by subscription with the medical professors becoming responsible to the subscribers to keep the building in repair and pay six percent for the money; the title to be in the Trustees' name. The building is to cost $1,000. It is now expected to open a law department next winter."[27] The medical faculty did not return in 1848 and the law department did not open.

A medical department catalogue was published for the 1848-1849 classes; however, there is no record of classes being held after the "Anniversary Exercises of the Medical College" on February 29, 1848. After the medical department closed in 1848, Samuel Adams continued teaching in the literary college while Henry Jones returned to his private practice in Jacksonville full time, occasionally teaching at the college. Edward Mead, who replaced Stahl in 1844, left to open a private facility for the insane in the Chicago area. Prince remained in Jacksonville for a few months and then moved to St. Louis for a teaching position.

In April 1848, soon after the department closed, the Illinois State Journal, *a Springfield newspaper, reported an unusual surgery performed by Prince: "Professor Prince removed from the shoulder of a lady, a few days since, while she was under influence of chloroform, a tumor eleven inches in circumference and weighing one pound and four ounces – The operation was entirely successful."*

Despite its brief existence, the Illinois College medical school contributed to an increase in the number of trained physicians and surgeons in Illinois. Of the approximately one hundred students who attended the department over five years, thirty graduated. Seventeen later practiced in Illinois, nine went west and the others to a variety of states. Five medical department graduates are on record as having served in the Civil War, three as soldiers and two as surgeons: Clark Roberts, First Illinois Infantry, and James S. Whitmire, Sixth Illinois Cavalry.[28]

Illinois College's Medical Department was the first medical school in Illinois; it opened in November 1843, one month before Rush Medical College in Chicago, which now holds the title of oldest continuous medical school in Illinois. The *History of*

Medical Practice in Illinois (1927) notes that the Illinois College Medical Department "was better equipped than Rush or Franklin medical colleges. Rush had the good fortune to have had a better geographical location and accordingly received greater support as a consequence."[29]

ENDNOTES

[1] Rammelkamp, Charles Henry. *Illinois College A Centennial History 1829-1929.* 1928.

[2] Black, Carl E. "A Pioneer Medical School." *Illinois Medical Journal.* January3, 1913. 12, Footnote.

[3] Black, Carl E. "Illinois' First Medical School." *Early American Medical Schools.* Vol. 1 Chicago. 1934. 248.

[4] Yeager, Iver F., *Julian M. Sturtevant 1805-1886/ President of Illinois College, Ardent Churchman, Reflective Author.* Jacksonville. The Trustees of Illinois College. 1999. 234.

[5] Yeager, Iver F., *Julian M. Sturtevant 1805-1886. 96.*

[6] Black. "A Pioneer Medical School." 24.

[7] Black. "A Pioneer Medical School." 18.

[8] Black. "A Pioneer Medical School." 11.

[9] Black. "A Pioneer Medical School." 24.

[10] Black. "A Pioneer Medical School." 25.

[11] Weaver, George Howlett. *Beginnings of Medical Education in and near Chicago.* 17; Sturtevant, J. M. *A Memorial Sketch of Samuel Adams.* 4; Duncan, Elizabeth. "Diary of Mrs. Joseph Duncan." Journal of the Illinois State Historical Society. Vol. 21, No. 1. April 1928.

[12] Sappol, Michael. *A Traffic of Dead Bodies.* Princeton and Oxford: Princeton University Press. 2002. 106.

[13] Norbury, Frank B. "David Prince/Pioneer Surgeon." *Illinois Medical Journal.* May 1966.

[14] Black. "A Pioneer Medical School." 13.

[15] Black. "A Pioneer Medical School." 11-12, Footnote 5.

[16] Kampmeier. Otto F. "History of Anatomy Laws in Illinois During the 19th Century." Pages 368-369, 384.

[17] Palmer, John McAuley, M.D., Editor. The Bench and the Bar of Illinois Historical and Reminiscent. Chicago. The Lewis Publishing Company. 1899.

[18] Black. "A Pioneer Medical School." 11.

[19] Kampmeier, Otto F., M.D. "Medical Libraries in Illinois before 1900." *History of Medical Practice in Illinois.* The State Medical Society. The Lakeside Press. R. R. Donnelley & Sons. 1955. 457.

[20] Black. "Morgan County Medical Society Ships Library to College of Surgeons." *The Jacksonville Daily Courier.* Jacksonville, Illinois. July 5, 1941.

[21] Black. "Morgan County Medical Society Ships Library to College of Surgeons."

[22] "Morgan County Medical Society donation." American College of Surgeons. Special Collections: letters.

[23] "Morgan County Medical Society donation." American College of Surgeons.

[24] Author's conversation with ACS Archivist Susan Rishworth. Summer 2013.

[25] Julian Sturtevant to Theron Baldwin. March 30, 1847. Baldwin-Sturtevant Letters 1830-1870. Illinois College Schewe Library Archives.

[26] Rammelkamp. *Illinois College A Centennial History 1829-1929.* 1928. 1.

[27] Baldwin-Sturtevant Letters 1830-1870. Illinois College Schewe Library Archives.

[28] Jenkins, Carol S. "Shingles in the Wind, the Impact of the Illinois College Medical Department". Illinois College. Graduate Colloquium. 1985. Illinois College, Schewe Library Archives. 8.

[29] Zeuch, Lucius H., M.D. *History of Medical Practice in Illinois Preceding 1850. Vol. I.* 398.

V
Return to Jacksonville

"You see I am in Jacksonville again – My old residence before going to St. Louis – all things considered I like this better than St. Louis and better I suppose than I should like any city."
David Prince to Emily Thompson,
February 25, 1852

David Prince moved to St. Louis in March 1848 to teach anatomy at St. Louis Medical University. His wife Mary Jane (*nee* Dawson) died the following year. Their four very young children died earlier (three of the children had been born to Mary Jane and David; the fourth was the niece of Mary Jane). No documentation of these deaths is found in public records.

An outbreak of cholera started among immigrants in St. Louis in January 1849, then spread and hit epidemic proportions citywide. In a *St. Louis Post-Dispatch* article for July 2010, "A Look Back," reporter Tim O'Neil wrote: "By July, the city was recording a weekly death count of six hundred and forty. The July 1849 issue of *Missouri Republican* noted eighty-eight burials a day – not by name, only grouped by cemetery."[1]

Prince was appointed resident physician at the City Hospital that year and served until the cholera epidemic abated in August.[2] In addition to teaching part of the year, Prince worked at establishing a private practice. He joined the St. Louis Medical Society and was elected president in 1851.

The wider medical community also was starting to recognize Prince's surgical innovations, although Prince himself seems not to have sought applause for his work. Prince had invited a former student, Dr. Samuel Willard, to stay with him in St. Louis while Willard was setting up his own practice. "In 1850, when I roomed with him in St. Louis," Willard wrote later, "he received a medical journal which was English and mailed from England. He scanned its pages quickly to find something of interest, then tossed it to me saying, 'I don't see why anybody sent me that.' I found in it a short article which gave the names of the eight or ten persons who had up to that time successfully removed ovarian tumors; his name was there as of Payson, Illinois."[3]

In 1850, Prince documented an operation he had done in 1847 in an article for *The American Journal of the Medical Sciences*:

> *Mrs. Cooper, aged about twenty-five, complained in the beginning of 1846 of a sudden attack of pain in the abdomen from which she soon recovered after having been 'bled and blistered.' These attacks were repeated at irregular intervals, and soon the patient discovered by accident a tumor which she said moved readily from side to side in the intervals of the attacks of pain, but could not be removed during the painful paroxysms. This tumor, though sometimes larger than at others, gradually increased in size and became less movable, until it seemed to occupy a large portion of the abdomen lying upon the right side and projecting below, beyond the median line upon the left side, and extending from behind the pubis to the right hypochondriac region. As the tumor increased in size, the health became more continuously*

impaired and the painful paroxysms more frequently repeated. The catamenia (menstruation) *became irregular but not suppressed. In this latter stage, the tumor could be made to roll slightly, but this was painful. A simulation of fluctuation* (from rolling of the tumor) *appeared upon palpation from side to side, but none from pressure in the direction of the long axis of the tumor – from pubis to right hypochondrium.*

December 25, 1847, made an incision three inches in length in the linea alba (a fibrous structure that runs down the midline of the abdomen), *midway between the pubis and umbilicus, and found the anterior surface of the tumor adherent to the posterior surface of the anterior wall of the abdomen. A free incision was made in the substance of the tumor itself and a portion of its interior removed. This appeared very much like the substance of the spleen as seen after death, but the small amount of blood lost from this surface indicated very little vascularity. A few minute hydatids* (cysts) *were discovered, as the result of a breaking down of the structure of the tumor by means of a probe passed freely in various directions through the tumor. A large amount of pus and for a long time was discharged, prostrating the patient, but generous diet, wine and quinine enabled the system to rally from this state, and to outlast the final removal of the tumor and the cessation of suppuration.*

June 16, 1849. The husband of the patient writes, "My wife is now well and hearty, and I have the gratifying news to tell you that we have a fine healthy daughter born upon the tenth of April last."[4]

While in St. Louis, Prince met several professional colleagues. One of the most enduring relationships was with Dr. John T. Hodgen, a demonstrator in the anatomy department when Prince started teaching at St. Louis Medical University. Hodgen graduated from that university the previous year. He later contributed to many medical journals and was one of the founders of the American Surgical Association. He served as president of the American Medical Association in 1881. Prince and Hodgen became life-long friends, personally and professionally.

After the Civil War, both physicians were among the early and few adherents of the "Germ Theory." Joseph Lister had published two papers in 1867 on the antiseptic principle in the *Lancet* and the *British Medical Journal*. In 1876, Lister presided over a section of the International Medical Congress in Philadelphia. The section began with an address by Hodgen on "Antiseptic Surgery" that supported Lister's work. There were American surgeons who expressed disagreement with Hodgen's address. When Lister spoke, he credited Pasteur's work in microbiology for the development of antiseptic surgery.[5]

Upon returning to his practice in Jacksonville in late 1851, Prince rejoined his friends at Illinois College and the Congregational Church. He became fully involved in state and local political issues and participated in the recently chartered Illinois State Medical Society.

Abolition supporters had been active in Jacksonville in the 1830s and became more vigorous in participating in the Underground Railroad after the November 1837 murder of publisher Elijah P. Lovejoy in Alton. Lovejoy died while he was defending his newspaper office against pro-slavery rioters. He had been celebrated in Jacksonville when he spoke at Illinois College and the Congregational Church, "the Abolition Church," about his abolitionist advocacy and his championing freedom of the press and freedom of speech. Among the anti-slavery leaders in Jacksonville were Prince's close friends Jonathan Baldwin Turner and Dr. Samuel Adams. The Underground Railroad operated in Springfield as well, but Springfield was not the abolition hotbed that existed in Jacksonville.

Entrances to Illinois for run-away slaves were usually the Mississippi River ports of Chester, Alton, and Quincy. Most of the runaway slaves who reached Alton came to Jacksonville, where they found a brief refuge and passage further north to Chicago.[6]

According to his granddaughter, Prince participated in the Underground Railroad. Mary Prince Richardson wrote to Prince biographer Dr. Frank Norbury in November 1965: "His house was a station on the 'underground railroad' and he moved the escaped slaves to Chandlerville while supposedly making a night call. There, the next station on the underground railroad for Prince was at the house of Dr. Charles Chandler."[7]

Chandler had immigrated to Illinois in 1832 from West Woodstock, Connecticut, stopping in Beardstown, Illinois because the second Black Hawk War created safety concerns about going further north. Within a year, he moved sixteen miles east to Panther Creek. He purchased land and encouraged development of the area by donating lots for schools and for three churches – Presbyterian, Congregational, and Methodist. The village grew to thirty households by 1851, when the village was incorporated as Chandlerville.

Prince and Chandler became acquainted when Chandler was appointed to evaluate candidates for medical degrees from the Illinois College Medical Department. They shared a scientific interest in preventive medicine and in prescribing quinine. During his trips to the Chandler home, Prince became acquainted with Chandler's niece, Lucy Manning Chandler of Fredonia, New York. She was the daughter of Charles' eldest brother John. Lucy had come to join her two cousins, who were attending Monticello Female Seminary in Godfrey, Illinois. Lucy attended for two years, also tutoring younger students, and graduated in 1850 at the age of twenty-four.[8] The relationship of David and Lucy bloomed, according to a letter Prince sent to his cousin Emily Thompson in Connecticut dated February 25, 1852:

I received a letter from my sister Mary a few days ago saying that all were well in Payson – that letter had recently been received from you making inquiries with regards to Lucy and extend an invitation to visit. These inquiries and this invitation she very properly transmitted to me, which according to your request or of her own accord – more likely the latter and I thank you most cordially for the kind remembrance of your cousin David.

Well, I continue to think a great deal of Miss Lucy and you need not be surprised of marriage in May!! It would be a great gratification to visit you especially as her own relatives now live in Connecticut. But we shall be 'young folks' just beginning you know and I doubt whether a prudent judgement would justify the time it will take, for if we should go to New England at all we could not be satisfied without going all along the shore.

You see I am in Jacksonville again – My old residence before going to St. Louis – all things considered I like this better than St. Louis and better I suppose than I should like any city.

I must extract from you the promise that when Lucy and I get to 'housekeeping' you will come and make us a visit.

My sister in-law Eliza (Dawson) is with me in Jacksonville and I suppose will continue to live here. For the last ten years she has been a member of my family or been a friend and sister and if she can be happy to share my Camp. And render such service as she knows so well how, as by making herself more independent of me. I shall be happier to retain her angelic presence.

My kindest regards to Uncle, Aunt and Cousins unknown except by tradition and with the hope of seeing them some day. My brother Edward who is here now in his senior year in college would be pleased to be remembered if he knew I was writing. For write me soon;

Your friend and cousin true David Prince"[9]

David and Lucy had a celebratory sendoff from Chandlerville and were married May 10, 1852 in Fredonia, New York. A year later, on April 15, 1853, David and Lucy purchased property at West State Street and South Fayette Street in Jacksonville. The purchase price was $1,600 to be paid in two years at ten percent interest. The lien was discharged November 14, 1855. A barn behind the house included a loft with a cupola that Prince reconstructed into a hidden loft for performing dissections.[10]

The couple had three children: Arthur Edward on April 3, 1854; Stella on April 3,1858; and John Abbott on October 30, 1863. The sons would both become surgeons and join their father in treating patients at the David Prince Sanitarium. Stella Prince Stocker married a physician and moved to Duluth, Minnesota. She pursued a career in music performance.

Following the marriage and settling in Jacksonville, Prince continued his private practice, as well as engaging in local political issues. He also continued active participation in the fledgling Illinois State Medical Society. In June 1852, Jacksonville and Morgan County physicians hosted the third annual meeting of the society at the Presbyterian Church, according to the *Illinois Daily Journal*, June 24, 1852. Officers were elected during the business portion of the meeting, and Prince was assigned as one of three members of the Committee on Surgery. Prince also was appointed to attend the second meeting of the American Medical Association the following year in New York. Jacksonville physicians arranged for the attendees to visit the School for the Deaf and Dumb, the State School for the Education of the Blind, and the State Hospital for the Insane. At the close of the two-day meeting, it was determined the next meeting would be in Chicago in June 1853.

Prince attended Congregational churches with his parents as a youth and joined the Congregational Church in Jacksonville when he first moved there in 1845. The church, established in 1835, is said to have been the first meeting house for Congregationalists in Illinois. Initially, meetings were in private homes until a church was constructed on the east side of the

Jacksonville square. In 1857, the church building was sold and the current church on West College Avenue constructed.

Establishment of the Congregational Church in Jacksonville led to breaking with Presbyterians on the Plan of Union, an agreement for organizing churches in the West, with Congregational ministers being called to established Presbyterian churches. Historian Frank Heinl writes: "This edifice, like the old New England meeting houses, became a center of community activities; lecturers in the church included Lyman and Henry Ward Beecher, Ralph Waldo Emerson, Bayard Taylor, Abraham Lincoln, Owen Lovejoy and other notables of the period. Musicales, lyceums and day schools were also held."[11]

Prince and Johnathan Baldwin Turner took the initiative to invite Ralph Waldo Emerson to lecture at the Congregational Church in Jacksonville on January 18, 1853. Prince and Turner were inspired when they learned Emerson was scheduled to lecture in St. Louis in December 1852 and in Springfield in January 1853. Emerson's topics were related to his version of Transcendentalism, in which he emphasized individualism and intellectual improvement. Prince and Turner wrote to him with a request to speak in Jacksonville after he completed the series in Springfield.

According to a list of correspondence in Emerson's "Pocket Diary," he responded affirmatively to Prince and Turner on January 8, 1853. In a letter to his wife, Lidian, he mentions he was going to Jacksonville. On January 11 he wrote his wife again: "Here I am in the deep mud of the prairie ..." He added details in his journal: "At Jacksonville, 35 miles, by strap-rail-road. I found an excellent man in David Prince and a man of much natural polemic talent in Johnathan Baldwin Turner."[12]

When Emerson arrived in Jacksonville, he stayed with rancher/farmer Jacob Strawn, whose wife was related to Emerson's wife. Emerson was quite impressed by Strawn and his landholdings – an estimated forty thousand acres – describing him as "a man of prodigious energy." He was also impressed by Elizur Wolcott, who was characterized by locals as the most erudite man in central Illinois. Wolcott was in charge of maintaining the railroad between Jacksonville and Springfield. Emerson commented: "… he in working clothes and is a graduate of Yale College."[13] The local newspaper made only brief mention of Emerson's lecture, referring to it as an "unimpassioned conversation," among other derogatory remarks.

Following the lecture, Prince took Emerson to visit a chemistry class at the high school, where molecules of hydrogen were called "blocks." Emerson commented: "These atoms are not square, but round: they are spherules of force." Prince reflected, "This seems to me a new way of looking at it and seemed to me a good way of getting it out of sight."[14]

Emerson lectured in the West throughout the 1850s, traveling to Ohio, Indiana, Illinois, Iowa, Michigan and Wisconsin, but he never returned to Jacksonville. In addition to bemoaning the mud, he found downstate Illinois accommodations poor, and "the people for the most part not 'thinking people."[15]

The Congregational Church, meanwhile, questioned whether Prince should remain a member. Samuel Adams, a former faculty colleague at the Illinois College Medical Department, presented a motion at the church's business meeting on September 12, 1855 to deny membership to Prince. Prince, Adams said, was no longer "in sympathy and cooperation with the statement of faith." Adams also claimed Prince did not provide the required documentation to transfer his membership to Jacksonville when he returned from St. Louis after an absence of more than two years. As a third point, Adams contended Prince did not regularly attend church services and other activities. (Details of the meetings are incomplete as the reproduction film record of the business meeting minutes is damaged, leaving it only partially legible.)[16]

Prince had joined the Jacksonville church in 1845 by letter from the Payson Congregational Church, where his father was an elder. Upon moving to St. Louis in 1848, he requested a letter be sent to the Park Congregational Church, but when he returned to Jacksonville, Prince said, he did not recall requesting or receiving a letter from the St. Louis church. Prince was permitted to respond to Adams' charges by letter. Drs. Maro Reed and Hiram Jones read the lengthy Prince letter. Among other responses, Prince wrote that his practice kept him from participating in many church activities. In addition to his Jacksonville patients, Prince was frequently called by physicians outside Morgan County to assist with difficult surgeries. In addition, he was a contract surgeon for the Sangamon and Morgan Rail Road.[17]

An undercurrent of Prince's relationship with the church is revealed by his granddaughter, Mary Prince Richardson, who wrote to a Prince biographer in 1965: "Dr. David accepted the Darwin Theory which did not please the Congregational Church." Richardson did not give further details.[18] When Charles Darwin's *Origin of Species* was published in 1859, it initiated an international debate. It was especially controversial for Congregationalists in England and America, because Darwin was a Congregationalist. The theory of evolution was seen as "materialistic." Adams wrote an article critical of Darwin's theory in 1871 for *The Congregational Review* under the title "Darwinism."

In Iver Yeager's biography of Julian M. Sturtevant, he noted: "In a lengthy rebuttal, Prince acknowledged that he would rejoice to see a wider latitude of doctrine allowed." Aside from being president of Illinois College, Sturtevant was a trustee of Jacksonville's Congregational Church and was active in state and national Congregational organizations. "No mention is made of any role by Sturtevant," Yeager concludes, "but it is unlikely that Adams would have acted without consulting him." A vote to revoke Prince's membership was followed by a minority protest by sixteen of the thirty-five members that led to reversing the decision.[19]

The Illinois State Medical Society was formally organized in Springfield in 1850, when Prince was still working in St. Louis. When he returned, he began regular attendance at annual meetings. Whenever Prince had an unusual surgery, he prepared a report for medical society discussion. (Member reports were often published in medical journals.)

Prince also built on other members' reports, as he was prompted to do in 1858, when he had a case relating to the use of iodine to cure a pleural cavity infection that was similar to a case reported earlier by Dr. Daniel Brainard of Rush Medical College. Prince's report was published in the *Chicago Medical Journal.* Prince wrote that an otherwise healthy four-year-old boy had an attack of pleuritis on the right side. His parents had depended on the illness to run its course. After six weeks, an enlargement appeared on the boy's right side, and he was able to breathe only when in a sitting position. Prince inserted a thin tube that led to "immediate and inexpressible relief" following a discharge of "a considerable quality of pus." Two weeks later, a second puncture was followed by daily draining of pus. However, Prince noted, "nature seemed not to be making progress." At that point, Prince began to use iodine as recommended in articles by Brainard. "On the 25th of March, two drachms of strong tincture of iodine were thrown in by a small glass syringe." The discharge abated after five injections about a week apart. Prince concludes his report: "The respiratory murmur could be heard throughout the whole extent of the lung; all sign of disease had disappeared, and by the middle of May the boy was at play with his top."[20]

After Prince treated the young boy, he reported another difficult surgery to the state medical society. The report was published in *The American Journal of Medical Sciences*. Prince was presented with Martha Walker, a sixty-year-old Black woman, who had had a tumor growing on her left salivary gland for forty years. The gland extended from the ear to the usual position of the mouth. Prince surmised that damage to the facial nerve caused paralysis of muscles on the sound side of the mouth that led to it be drawn up.

"The patient has for a long time suffered great pain in and around the tumor, and has had ague (a term for malaria) during the autumn, and looks in a miserable condition." Several days before surgery, Prince recruited four physicians and medical students to assist him. During that time the woman's stomach was purged in preparation for surgery, and she was administered whisky and quinine during the day and morphia at night. Immediately before surgery she was given an ounce of whisky and a quarter grain of morphia; then she was "stupefied with a sufficient quantity of ether and chloroform." Assisting Prince in the operation from Jacksonville were: Drs. Hiram K. Jones, M.M.L. Gaddis, William Edgar, O. H. Knight and Dr. William Jayne of Springfield. Medical students attending were studying with Prince before entering medical college.[21]

Surgery began with a zig-zag incision, leaving several square inches of skin on the tumor. Forceps were inserted into the tumor and handed to an assistant to lift the tumor from attachments, which were cut or tied off if likely to hemorrhage. After the tumor was removed every visage of disease was removed. "The amount of blood lost was not great, and the operation was attended with fewer difficulties than had been anticipated."

A three-week history of the patient's recovery reports that she was able to swallow at bedtime the day of the surgery. Her incision was tended daily, with the wound diminishing by half by the twenty-first day. Her pulse was 120 on the second day. Pulse had declined to 80 by the fifth day. Walker was up and walking briefly on the fifth day, as well as taking nourishment; by the twelfth day, she was described as having a good appetite and by the twenty-first day "takes freely of rich food." After the twenty-first day, the only care was treating the wound until healed. "From this time, she went on very well."[22]

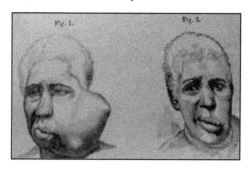

Figure 1: A Prince woodcut of patient Martha Walker before and after facial surgery.

In addition to his practice during this period, Prince also was active in the Illinois State Medical Society. At the annual meeting held in Bloomington on June 5, 1855, Prince and other members initiated an effort to establish what became the Asylum for the Education of Feeble- Minded Children. Prince gave a report on the need of an institution for a class of children referred to as "idiots" or "imbeciles." He, along with Drs. J.V.Z. Blaney of Chicago and E.R. Roe of Bloomington, were appointed to draft a memorial to the legislature regarding establishing an "institution for idiots." The committee continued its assignment for four years amid other topics assigned.[23]

However, the memorial did not get legislative attention until a decade later. After the Civil War, State Sen. Murray McConnel of Jacksonville introduced and shepherded a bill that came into force February 16, 1865, "An Act to organize an experimental school for the instruction and training of idiots and feeble-minded children." Advocates for the school were able to convince legislators this would be an experimental school for training and teaching at a cost no more than if the same children were enrolled in other institutions. Lawmakers approved the bill with an appropriation of five thousand dollars.[24]

The experimental school was established by renting former Gov. Joseph Duncan's vacant mansion and grounds, one block away from the school for the deaf. The school opened May 25, 1865, with three children; enrollment grew to eighty children by 1871. That year, the experimental school was incorporated by the legislature and named the Institution for the Education of Feeble-Minded Children. Three trustees were appointed by the governor: Prince, Graham Lee of Mercer County and Timothy Souther of Madison County.[25]

The report of 1871 by trustees Prince and Lee said the institution had demonstrated that feeble-minded children could be educated. It elaborated testimony by parents and friends that "their children have, under the training of the institution, improved in health and in personal appearance; are less nervous, less awkward, and more active." The comments also noted: "They are found to be less troublesome at home, talk more and more distinctly, comprehend language more readily, use a greater variety of words and more connected sentences."[26]

In 1875, the legislature appointed a board of commissioners to select a permanent location. The city of Lincoln was selected. The Asylum for Feeble Minded Children opened there in 1878 with a new board of trustees.[27]

In 1860, Prince was elected president of the Illinois State Medical Society. In his inaugural address, he introduced a new topic for consideration; medico-legal issues. Prince described the doctor's dilemma of being sued for malpractice or arrested for performing dissections to improve his knowledge and skill. Malpractice suits were proliferating throughout the state, he said, most often because patients had been dissatisfied with their recovery after fractures. "The medical witnesses are often bitter enemies to members of their own profession, and lawyers delight in playing the doctors off against each other."[28]

Prince advocated the licensing of trained doctors through a state-appointed Board of Medical Assessors "of men in high repute in their respective departments." It would be more than fifteen years before the Illinois General Assembly would approve a Board of Medical Assessors.

ENDNOTES

[1] O'Neil, Tim. "A look back – Cholera epidemic hit here in 1849" *St. Louis Post-Dispatch.* July 18, 2010.

[2] Sharf, J. Thomas. *History of Saint Louis City and County, From the Earliest Periods to the Present Day. Vol. 2.* Philadelphia. Louis H. Everts & Company. 1883.

[3] Black, Carl E. M.D. "Illinois' First Medical School." *Illinois Medical Journal. Vol. XXIII.* Springfield, IL. January, 1913. 24, note 21.

[4] Prince, David, M.D. "Solid Ovarian Tumour, extending from Pubis to right Hypochondrium - Cured by Incision followed by Suppuration." *The American Journal of the Medical Sciences, Vol. XX.* 267-268.

[5] Shastid. *My Second Life.* 160-161; 170-171.

[6] Heinl, Frank J. "Jacksonville and Morgan County an Historical Review." *Journal of the Illinois State Historical Society (1908-1984).* Vol. 18, No.1. Champaign-Urbana. University of Illinois Press. 1925. 18-20.

[7] Mary Prince Richardson to Dr. Frank B. Norbury. November 1865. Norbury Papers. Jacksonville (IL) Public Library. Richardson was a granddaughter of David and daughter of Arthur E. Prince.

[8] Chandler, Josephine Craven. "Dr. Charles Chandler: His Place in the American Scene." *Journal of the Illinois State Historical Society.* Vol. 24, No. 3 (Oct., 1931) pp. 369-552. University of Illinois Press on behalf of the Illinois State Historical Society. URL: http://www.jstor.org/stable/40187747.

[9] David Prince to Emily Thompson. "Scarborough Family Papers." Held by Jared Scarborough, Payson, Illinois. With permission of Mr. Scarborough.

[10] Records of the Chautauqua County, New York, County Historian; Records Office of the Morgan County Clerk, Jacksonville, Illinois.

[11] Heinl, Frank J. "Congregationalism in Jacksonville and Early Illinois." *Journal of the Illinois State Historical Society.* Vol. 25, No. 4. (January 1935). 442.

[12] Emerson, Ralph Waldo. *The Journals and Miscellaneous Notebooks of Ralph Waldo Emerson, Vol. VXIII.* Editors: Ralph H. Orth and Alfred R. Furguson. Cambridge. The Belknap Press. 1977.351. Illinois State Library.

[13] Seybold, Ethel. "Transcendentalism Comes to Jacksonville." *Jacksonville Journal Courier.* October 21, 1981. Section B 37-40. Prior to her passing in 2005, Seybold was Professor Emeritus at Illinois College, English Department.

[14] Seybold.

[15] Seybold.

[16] Congregational Church Record of Business Meetings. Illinois College Schewe Library, Special Collections.

[17] Congregational Church Record of Business Meetings.

[18] Mary Prince Richardson to Dr. Frank B. Norbury. November 1965. Norbury papers. Jacksonville (IL) Public Library. Special Collections.

[19] Yeager, Iver F., *Julian M. Sturtevant 1805-1886/ President of Illinois College, Ardent Churchman, Reflective Author.* Jacksonville. The Trustees of Illinois College. 1999. 183. The late Iver Yeager was former Dean of Illinois College and Professor of Religion and Philosophy. He was also Archivist for the Congregational Church.

[20] Prince, David, M.D. "Empyema Treated by Injections." *The Chicago Medical Journal*, Vol.1. 1858.

[21] Prince. "Extripation of the Parotid Gland." Philadelphia. *The American Journal of the Medical Sciences.* Blanchard and Lea. 1860. 57.

22 Prince. "Extripation of the Parotid Gland. 60.

23 "History of the Asylum for Feeble Minded Children." *Brief History of the Charitable Institutions of the State of Illinois.* Committee on State Charitable Institutions of the Illinois Board of World's Fair Commissioners. Chicago.1893. 3.

24 "An Act to organize an experimental school for the instruction and training of idiots and feeble-minded children in Illinois." Public Laws of the State of Illinois passed by Twenty-Fourth General Legislature convened January 2, 1865. 78-79.

25 History of the Asylum for Feeble Minded Children." *Brief History of the Charitable Institutions of the State of Illinois.*

26 *Seventh Annual Report of the Institution for the Education of Feeble-Minded Children.* Jacksonville, Illinois. December 1871. 7-8. The report noted that while entitled as the "Seventh Annual Report" it was the first report for these trustees. It was signed by Graham Lee and David Prince, Timothy Souther having died after his appointment and before taking office.

27 History of the Asylum for Feeble Minded Children." *Brief History of the Charitable Institutions of the State of Illinois.*

28 Davis, David J., Editor. *History of Medical Practice in Illinois Vol. II: 1850-1900.* Chicago. The Illinois State Medical Society. R. R. Donnelley & Sons. 1955. 49.

VI
Civil War Surgeon

"I am personally acquainted with Dr. Prince, and know him to be of excellent private character, and a Surgeon of the highest reputation."

Abraham Lincoln to Simon Cameron,
Secretary of War, June 4, 1861

In the year before the Civil War broke out, David Prince was settled into a medical practice that reached beyond Jacksonville, as he was often called outside Morgan County for difficult surgeries. In addition, he was a contract surgeon for the Sangamon and Morgan Rail Road. His family included a six-year-old son and a two-year-old daughter. Active in community organizations, Prince also was elected president of the Illinois State Medical Society in 1860. Jacksonville had grown in population to 5,528, according to the 1860 census.

In March of 1860, the Quincy Guard, a militia unit, passed through Jacksonville homeward bound from the funeral of Gov. William Henry Bissell in Springfield. They stopped to visit the grave of Col. John J. Hardin, who had died in 1847 at the battle of Buena Vista, Mexico. The Quincy Guard was led by Colonels John Morgan and Benjamin Prentiss, who were with Hardin when he was killed. A week after this event, Jacksonville young men began forming military companies, the first of which was the Hardin Light Guard.[1]

More volunteers enlisted in late April 1861, following the fall of Fort Sumter. The Union Guard elected James Dunlap as captain, and the Hardin Light Guard elected Charles Adams as captain. Joining the Hardin Light Guard was the entire senior class of Illinois College. All the students were granted degrees before leaving. These two units and one from Quincy were sent to Cairo, where they were organized into the 10th Illinois Infantry. In 1862, the unit was attached to the command of Gen. Ulysses Grant. Prince's brother, Col. Edward Prince of Quincy, was commissioned by Governor Richard Yates in September 1861 to lead the 7th Illinois Cavalry.[2]

Volunteer companies from Morgan County trained at Camp Duncan, a mile west of the Jacksonville village square. After training, the companies were formed into the 14th Illinois Infantry Regiment. Those attending a flag-raising ceremony at the camp on May 14, 1861 were shaken by an incident that brought home the risks of war. Ladies of Jacksonville were to present a flag to the regiment's officers. The companies formed ranks on three sides of a flagpole in front of the officers' headquarters. As the flag was raised, an old cannon was fired, and "during the act of reloading the second time, went off prematurely blowing both hands of one man entirely off." The man was taken to the nearby hospital at the State School for the Deaf, where Dr. Prince amputated the remains of the man's hands.[3]

> *The many friends of Dr. D. Prince will be pleased to learn that he has received an appointment as Brigade Surgeon in the army. It is not yet known to what brigade he will be attached. If this is a specimen appointment, the service is to be congratulated upon having secured the best surgical skill and medical proficiency of the country. We trust the Doctor will be attached to a brigade which will have active and not garrison*

duty to perform, as he would be in his element on the battle field.
Jacksonville Journal, August 29, 1861

President Lincoln's endorsement led to Prince's appointment on August 3, 1861 as a brigade surgeon with the rank of major. Lincoln wrote the recommendation on the back of a letter from Pittsfield physician Benjamin Norris to John Nicolay, Lincoln's private secretary. Nicolay had previously lived in Pittsfield, where he published a newspaper.[4]

Prince first went to Cairo, Illinois to help examine volunteers' physical fitness. Located at the confluence of the Ohio and Mississippi Rivers, Cairo was a strategic Union defensive position and launch site for western operations against the Confederacy, but its military campground was not a healthy area. Outside the flood protection levee was a muddy plain that raised the risk in summer of sickness from mosquitoes carrying malaria. Inside the levee, there was no military discipline regarding personal hygiene or sanitation. This resulted in filth, rat infestation, and ailments such as fever, diarrhea and dysentery. Additionally, children's diseases, including measles, mumps and scarlet fever, were a problem for young men who had not been exposed to them. "Among the Illinois regiments camped at Cairo in August 1861, the sick rate ranged from as low as 29 to as high as 143 percent," according to George Worthington Adams' *Doctors in Blue.*[5]

A letter from Dr. Prince says that all the Jacksonville boys at Cairo are in good health.
Jacksonville Journal, Wednesday, September 5, 1861

> *Dr. Prince left town on last Friday evening under orders to report to Gen. McClellan immediately. The Doctor could not be better suited than to see active service on the sacred soil.*
> Jacksonville Journal, Wednesday, September 12, 1861

Prince arrived in Washington, D.C. in the aftermath of the First Battle of Bull Run. He was assigned to General Lawrence P. Graham's Brigade, composed of five New York and Pennsylvania regiments, which in turn was part of the Army of the Potomac's IV Corps. As a volunteer, Prince worked with the United States Sanitary Commission, rather than with the Medical Department of the Army of the Potomac that was directed by surgeon Charles S. Tripler.

However, a presidential commission gave Prince more responsibilities than other brigade surgeons. As a commissioned officer, Prince also held the title of senior surgeon for Gen. Darius Couch's 1st Division. He was responsible for administrative work of the regimental surgeons and had some authority to make recommendations to line officers with the expectation they would be carried out. It appears that line officers did not always follow this procedure. Prince complained to Tripler. Tripler responded:

> *Headquarters Army of the Potomac*
> *Medical Director's Office*
> *Washington, September 20, 1861*
> *Graham's Brigade,*
> *Brigade Surgeon Prince,*
> *Sir: Your duplicate report, which was very properly made, has been received. The brigade commander will no doubt issue the proper orders*

to correct the evils which you represented. In relation to your complaint that the colonel of the thirty-eighth Pennsylvania Volunteers does not recognize your official relations to him, I have to say that those relations depend upon your commission from the President of the United States and not upon the recognition or non-recognition of any individual officer under the President's command.

Very respectfully, your obedient servant
Charles A. Tripler
Medical Director Army of the Potomac"[6]

Tripler expected brigade surgeons to improve medical service by drilling litter-bearers and bandsmen. In addition to his other duties, Prince trained litter-bearers in the proper method of transporting wounded men. As a volunteer, Prince was responsible to the Sanitary Commission for ordering camp supplies, food, medical supplies and for reporting on medical operations. The USSC was a voluntary organization that began in New York City after President Lincoln called for a militia of 75,000 troops. A group of physicians and socially prominent women from the Women's Central Relief Association of New York vowed to do what they could to support the volunteer regiments to "preserve health among men required to live together in large masses."

Leadership came from USSC president Rev. Henry Bellows, a leader in the Unitarian Church and relief organizer. Also leading the effort was Dr. Elisha Harris, who was familiar with the efforts of the English Sanitary Commission during the Crimean War of 1853-1856. Uppermost in their minds was that disease could kill as many soldiers as could bullets. The USSC's goal was to support the army in matters of hygiene and sanitation by providing "comfort, stores and nurses in aid of the medical staff." The USSC also operated field hospitals behind the battlefronts, a hospital at White House, Virginia, and general hospitals in Washington and other cities of the North. Although based in New York, where the Medical Bureau of the Army was headquartered, the U.S. Sanitary Commission organized across the nation.

When a USSC delegation went to Washington, members asked that the USSC be assigned to help volunteer units with sanitation and hygiene inspections, make recommendations and provide nurses for hospitals.[7] The USSC representatives received a polite but frosty response from military and political leaders. According to USSC historian Charles J. Stillé: "The perfect disinterestedness of their motives was a quality so rare in the moral atmosphere of Washington, as to suggest to those who had lived longest in it gave doubts as to its reality and genuineness. The Surgeon General and army officers felt at the very least the USSC would be a nuisance. The most severe response came from Tripler, who characterized the USSC as "sensational preachers, village doctors and volunteer women."[8]

When, after several meetings with military officials, the USSC delegation finally received a rejection from Surgeon General Clement A. Finley, they went to Lincoln. The President is said to have viewed the USSC as a "fifth wheel to the coach" since the army already had a Medical Bureau. Nevertheless, he heard the representatives' request and called in Finley. "These gentlemen," Lincoln said, "tell me that they have raised a large amount of money, and organized a parent organization and many subordinate societies throughout the loyal states to provide the soldier with comforts, with materials to preserve his health, to shelter him, to cure his wounds and diseases, which the regulations of the War Department do not permit your office to supply. They offer to do all this without cost to the government or any interference with the action of your department for the good order and discipline of the army, and you have declined the offer." Finley mumbled that regulations did not permit civilian interference, and he asserted that everything a sick or wounded soldier might want or need would be supplied by the War Department. Lincoln replied, "If that is all you can say, I think you will have to accept the offer."[9]

On June 9, 1861, the U.S. Sanitary Commission received official approval from President Lincoln and Secretary of War Simon Cameron. Among the commission's first actions was to inspect the volunteer camps in Washington. They found no drainage in the camps, and "no pretense of performing the ordinary police duties of a military camp." Soldiers lacked personal cleanliness, and while there was an abundance of beef and pork, by regulation, no green vegetables were issued. Cooking was noted as the subject most in need of instruction. "The consequence was that the army was generally believed to be in great danger of decimation by scurvy or dysentery." The inspection report pointed out many of the problems arising from "inexperience of officers and the consequent want of discipline among the men."[10]

Sanitary Commission concerns that camp conditions would affect regiments' fitness in battle were borne out during the Peninsula Campaign in southeastern Virginia. The malarial swamps of the peninsula, especially the White Oaks Swamp and the boggy Chickahominy River, added to the list of diseases. Many officers were lost or impaired by sickness, not the least of whom was Union Army commander Gen. George McClellan himself, who dealt with malarial fever during the Seven Days Battles. According to Frank R. Freemon in *Gangrene and Glory*, 40.5 percent of total troops in the Army of the Potomac in July 1862 were sick or wounded – the vast majority of them victims of illness, not the Confederacy.[11]

The USSC also began purchasing stores and arranging for warehousing in New York and Washington. However, it wasn't until September 1862 at Antietam that the USSC was able to deploy supplies to battle zones. The army itself had problems getting sufficient ammunition to the battle. None of the essential medical supplies were available until a week after the battle, when a USSC wagon train delivered "28,763 pieces of dry goods, shirts, towels, bed-ticks and pillows; 30 barrels of old linen bandages and lint; 3,188 pounds of farina; 2,600 pounds of condensed milk; 5,000 pounds of beef stock and canned meat; several tons of lemons and other fruit, crackers, tea, sugar, tin cups and 120 bales of blankets."[12]

USSC inspections of twenty camps of volunteers around Washington were ongoing when the First Battle of Bull Run was fought on July 21, 1861. After the disastrous Union defeat, the USSC prepared a thoroughgoing report of interviews with many officers and men involved in the battle. Among the questions asked were "the strength of the regiments, their last meal, the degree of vigor before the battle and causes of exhaustion before it began." The commission's general conclusion was that the battle "proved the existence of some of the highest qualities of the soldier among the volunteers, but the disgraceful rout and confusion with which it ended, caused by a panic and a delusion and the utter demoralization which followed it, showed plainly that the most brilliant courage in battle may be rendered wholly useless by radical defects in organization and discipline."[13]

The USSC asked for an "Ambulance Regiment" to be formed under McClellan's command to increase the number of ambulances with trained drivers, as well as soldiers detailed as nurses for special care of the sick and wounded. McClellan denied the requests on the grounds that it had never been done before. In addition, the USSC questioned the number and size of the army's general hospitals. At the time, military hospitals were post hospitals, the largest of which was Fort Leavenworth with but forty beds. The USSC called for creating an entire system with suitable buildings, trained staff, an improved diet for the sick, clothing, a means of supplying medicines promptly and arrangement for humane transport of the sick and wounded. The commission said the army's Medical Bureau had failed to comprehend what was needed for a large army, such as a proper relationship between regimental hospitals and general hospitals.[14]

Prince arrived in Washington in September 1861. His after-battle report on the Peninsula Campaign the following spring describes earlier battles leading up to the Army of the Potomac leaving Washington to establish a base in preparation for the Siege of Yorktown. The description is punctuated with Prince's pointed opinions of the Union officers and his enmity towards West Point officers, especially General McClellan. Prince refers to a large section of his report as "Medical notes of the Peninsular Campaign 1862" and cautions the reader that the notes "are unfit to denote the movements of the armies."

Prince kept a personal diary of his activities during the war. Prince biographer Carl E. Black reports, the diary "was the property of the Library of Morgan County Medical Society, but some admiring friend has borrowed it and forgotten to leave his address."[15]

The reports below were prepared by Prince after he returned to Jacksonville. In addition to the Peninsula Campaign reports, Prince submitted other documents describing battlefield surgical procedures performed by him and others. Also, he submitted letters to his Sanitary Commission contact, Dr. Elisha Harris, about his travels in states to inspect military hospitals.

The Peninsula Campaign

The following excerpts focus on medical aspects of the campaign, skipping over Prince's criticism of military blunders made by McClellan and other generals. Prince reports to the USSC:

During January and February1862 we were fairly and snugly in winter quarters in huts, or tents with stoves and all the routine which makes the military vocation a busy life in peace as well as in time of war.

The crowning fault of the Medical administration during this period was the want of attention to ventilation. The men were allowed to shut themselves up in their tents and cabins very much as they pleased, in ignorance of the danger of poisoning themselves with foul air of their own production. The result was a great amount of typhoid or intestinal fever from the crowd poisoning and of pneumonia from the sudden transition from the sweating dens to the air of winter as they came out for roll call and other purposes.

The Medical officers were for the most part ignorant of the true conditions of military hygiene, and nearly all the information imparted on this subject came through the agents of the Sanitary Commission. It is difficult for medical men to shake off habits of civil practice in which there is not much demand for attention to preventative measures. They expect to admit the sick when they are sent for, and they are accustomed to think their duties are thus ended.

The whole army was taken down to Ft. Monroe to commence the campaign of the Peninsula so called from the naming of the strip of land between the James River on the south & west and Chesapeake Bay and York River on the north and east. For this purpose, Steam boats, Ships, Schooners and casual boats were deployed by the government from the Chesapeake, the Delaware Bay and from the harbors of N. York and Boston. The war power might have taken boats enough to transport the whole army, at one voyage but instead of this, the same boats went back and forth on separated trips before the whole army had been transported. So little calculation was made that in some instance's troops were ordered out of comfortable quarters to remain for three days in the mud at Alexandria waiting for boats in which to go to Ft. Monroe. All this miscalculation tended to diminish the efficiency of the army partly by laying the grounds of future sickness remitting.

This would have been felt if the campaign had been immediately commenced but the very considerable delay allowed the men to recover from the shock except those predisposed to rheumatism and those with incipient (knee tendonitis). This was a crisis to many of them and resulted in them being left at Washington or discharged in the early part of the campaign. The small amount of sickness engendered by voyage to Ft. Monroe is a good illustration of the protecting influence of change from monotony, and the excitement of expectation in relation to the causation of disease. The passage was too short to engender fear to any small extent by the infirmities accumulating unavoidably and this atmospheric contamination.

Great preparation was made to attack Yorktown with siege guns but when full preparations were nearly completed the rebels retreated and the siege guns were then of no use. On Sunday the 4th of May our General found out the evacuation and our forces followed after the enemy over taking them east of Williamsburg.

There was an unnecessary amount of fever produced chiefly through the instinct of protection from the cold in violation of the necessity prudence. The want of the latter comes to be appreciated only through experience while the demand for warmth is immediate and imperative. A practice came upon the men like an epidemic of constructing a kennel just large enough for two men to crawl into, the roof of which was made of the rubber blankets of the two men. All holes for the entrance of fresh air were stopped except that at which the men crowded in and asked that would be closed by a curtain made of an overcoat or thin garment. These were the elements of crowd poisoning without the crowd. It is obvious enough that the near enclosure of our men is as impossible as the crowding of a great number into a room with a space large absolutely but relatively the same.

Upon the march of the army after the evacuation of Yorktown numerous cases of advanced typhoid fever men pulled out of their holes, the lax discipline permitting the medical officers to remain in ignorance of their condition. After the battle of Williamsburg on May 5, 1862, the wounded were too quickly moved away to afford a satisfactory study for the medical officer traveling with the Army. Having only to be carried in ambulances from here 4 miles to comfortable transports, they were quickly sent to the Hospital North. No system of control of the ambulances existed but the absence of the enemy left the machinery to run itself without much entanglement; all the ambulances being ordered duty in carrying the wounded from the temporary hospitals to the York River after which the ambulances rejoined their specified regiments.[16]

Whiskey rations

During the Siege of Yorktown in April and early May, Medical Director Tripler suspended what had been the routine issuance of whiskey, brandy, and wine to soldiers. Prince notes: "A liberal amount of whisky was supplied from the departments of the Commissary the medical department having almost no stimulants. While at the Siege of Yorktown an order came from the Medical Director of the Army C.S. Tripler suspending the issue of Brandy, Whisky, and Wine by the Purveyor, requiring that before a battle, the articles should be placed in the keeping of the Senior Medical Officers of Divisions. No such notice of this approach of a battle however was ever given."[17]

After the Army of the Potomac advanced to within ten miles of Richmond and McClellan was positioning his forces for attack, army headquarters issued Special Order No. 52 on May 19, 1862. The order recommended reinstatement of the whiskey ration: "an extra ration of one gill of whiskey daily, will be issued until further orders to every officer and soldier in this army; half to be served out in the morning and half in the evening."[18]

Within two weeks, surgeons of IV Corps were telling Tripler that "the whiskey ration has proved a source of mischief instead of relief." The whiskey doses did nothing to reduce the prevalence of diarrhea and dysentery, they reported, to say nothing of malarial sickness. In addition, when the whiskey ration was available to officers and soldiers, it was not always available to surgeons, leaving them without stimulants for the sick and wounded. Whiskey was also blended with quinine to reduce the bitterness when quinine was administered to treat malarial fevers, a common practice in civilian medicine.

Prince wrote Tripler summarizing the discussions of surgeons in his division regarding the whiskey ration. Surgeons from other units were sending similar reports to Tripler, including Frank H. Hamilton, medical director of IV Corps, and T. R. Spencer, a division medical director. Spencer emphasized that in his opinion whiskey caused increased bowel afflictions and he had never seen an example of a cure from the use of whiskey. Included in Prince's communications with Tripler were his personal objections:

> *The ration is given without discrimination between those who need it and those who do not. The army ration of food, though faulty in kind, is more than sufficiently nutritious for men who have good digestion, and especially so for men who are lying idle in camp. From the nature of the case, the men will be most likely to get the whiskey ration when idle in the camp; while, upon the march, when it might be claimed to be useful to the more feeble portion of the men, they will not have it; and in the end of a forced march the supply will be very certain not to be at hand.*

From principles of health and endurance, well enough appreciated when applied to horses, it is known that over-stimulation in periods of inactivity is unfavorable to the greatest activity and endurance in periods immediately subsequent. If this is true, it must be obvious that the whiskey ration, as it must be given under this order, must be most mischievous to the health and endurance of the army, over stimulating the men when they are inactive, and failing to be at hand when exhaustion from fatigue might make it useful.

It is believed that whiskey has no power of preventing or curing disease arising from residence near marshy ground, except as it counteracts exhaustion from fatigue; and if so, the whiskey ration, from its indiscriminate use while inactive, favoring subsequent fatigue, which is will not be at hand to relieve, fails any useful end, and is on the contrary, in the main, hurtful. While all considerations of future health and usefulness in the soldier must be made subsidiary to his immediate military efficiency, it must be unfortunate to institute unnecessarily a routine of stimulation which makes the soldier a victim to the habit through life."[19]

On June 19, 1862, one month to the day after Special Order No. 32 was promulgated, Gen. McClellan discontinued the extra issue of whiskey. Commanding officers were directed to "enforce existing orders directing that hot coffee be served to the troops immediately after reveille." No reason was given for the change.[20]

The communications between Tripler and the IV Corps surgeons took place a few days prior to the Seven Pines Battle of May 31 and June 1. Prince was at the field hospital established at Savage's Station, two miles behind the Seven Pines battle line. The battle ended at a standstill, with both sides claiming victory and withdrawing from the battle lines. Both sides sustained comparable numbers of casualties – 1,132 Confederate, 1,203 Union.[21]

After the battle of Fair Oaks, Prince reported on gunshot wounds to the chest to Lt. Col. Frank H. Hamilton, chief surgeon for the 1st Long Island Volunteers. Prince reported "in several instances bullets were arrested by breastplates." Hamilton comments on the report: "In one case a breastplate was penetrated by a minié rifle-ball, but its force was so nearly expended after perforating the metallic plate, that it merely entered beneath the skin; and then passing along superficially over the muscular walls of the abdomen, it was found lying beneath the integument upon the opposite side."[22]

FIGURE 2: *Savage's Station Hospital, Virginia. Library of Congress. Photographer, James F. Gibbson, June 30, 1862.*

Change of base

Prince found no improvement in treatment of the wounded following the battle of Seven Pines:

> *I have spoken of the incompetence of the Quartermaster of this Army. There was no system or foresight in the processing regard for wounded men by the Medical officers in subordinate positions did what their ingenuity or foresight enabled them. Our Medical Director, Surgeon Tripler had a special spite against sick men. Men he said had no business to get sick in camp they might be prudent and take care of themselves.*
>
> *While sending off the wounded from this battle twenty miles by R.R. and thence by boats are mixed the sick men in with the wounded and thus evaded the orders of Dr. Tripler but after the wounded were all away, we could practice this game no longer.*
>
> *Rebel Gen. Stewart (sic – Confederate cavalry commander Gen. J.E.B. Stuart) made a raid upon the railroad in our rear between us and our boats to warn us of the uncertainty of our communication with our boats but all without opening the eyes of our Medical Director. He declared the hospital boats should be left for the wounded in the next battle. Our camp had sick men in the churches and houses by the wayside that were filed with patients with typhoid fever and chronic dysentery – boats were waiting idle at the distance of twenty miles with a R. R. intervening, and we were not allowed to send those men off. The poor fellows, I afterward saw*

*some of them in Richmond lying in filth devoured
by lice for the boats came and with them an enemy
in our rear.*

*It is not strange that military officers should
be impatient of the care necessary for sick and
wounded, but when this vice attaches to Medical
officers it becomes truly execrable. An instance of
this military impatience occurred after the Battle
of Seven Pines May 31. The principal depot of
wounded men had been made at a free house with
shaded yard on the R. R. about two miles in rear
of the battle field. The most shaded part of the
ground had been occupied by the tents of Gen.
Heintzleman (sic – Gen. Samuel Heintzelman)
and his staff. During Sunday the day after the
battle the Medical officers were permitted to do
what they could for the men in the front yard, but
the next morning the men were all ordered into
the back yard a Lieutenant alleging that the sight
of the men was offensive to the General! – Who is
this Gen. Heintzleman? A native of Pa, a graduate
of West Point, who has been many years on the
frontier fighting Indians assimilating himself to
the savage scenes around him.*

After further inconclusive fighting, McClellan ordered the
Army of the Potomac to withdraw from the peninsula in early
July. Prince, however, misled by earlier optimistic reports, was
expecting a Union advance.

*In full belief of this report I returned with my
attendants to my tent two miles in rear of the front,
the scenes which I have been describing about
midnight and expecting an active day, arose as
soon as there was light enough to see, and on*

looking out over the field could see a deserted hospital tent and a suttlers tent which was still standing because the team which should carry it was away. I awoke the Brigade Commissary sleeping in his tent near me who was intirely ignorant of what had taken place. On another part of the field piles of provisions, tents and everything that would burn were on fire and the men who were executing that distruction could only say that it was orders. The headquarters tents of the brigade of the division and of the Corps had all disappeared in the night. I soon found a quartermaster who told me that a movement to the James River had been odered and he knew the road the forces had taken.

Here were our sick men who had been denied transportation to the North – what should we do with them? In ignorance of the suspension of R.R. communications with White House we got the men to the railroad. A clearing about a mile from the RR by a beautiful spring was emptied of the sick men who were conveyed in ambulences to the RR to be sent away. The poor fellows, those of them that lived through those hardships went to Richmond and that was not the end of their troubles.

The right wing of McClellan's army then retreated across the Chickahominy River, destroying bridges, artillery and what Prince called "immense stores of provisions in the process."

The wounded and the sick made a motlay (sic) picture in this movement. If they went too fast they were in danger of being any movement in the midst of a battle and if they went too slow they were liable to be overtaken by the pursing enemy. They were continually asking questions when they should go but no one could tell them. The best advise I could give them was to keep as near their friends and acquantances as possible. Those who could walk got away. Those who could not mostly fell into the hands of the enemy. From Richmond to the James River there was very little transportation for the sick and wounded. The regimental surgeons required their ambulances for the necessities of the regiment upon the march, and no army wagons could be appropriated to this purpose for they were loaded with Quartermaster and Commissary Stores.

A strange order then appeared over the Authority of Gen. McClellan (probably written by Tripler) forbidding sick men to leave the ranks under penalty of being fired upon. This order was certainly in stricking contrast with the soldiers returning down the James River from Richmond a few weeks later and the tender inquires after their welfare by the General in Command as he visited the hospital boats during their temporary halt opposite the camp the army at Harrison's Landing.

Prince himself came under fire during the ensuing battle of Malvern Hill, the last of the Seven Days Battles, which took place July 1. His notes continue:

During the forenoon, the fight was almost exclusively one of artillery the rebels opening from sides of the field so that we could never know from what direction a shell could come. So little did we who were the uninitiated surgeons know of the plan of the battle that we were about raising a red flag at the gateway leading to a house in rear of our men nearly half a mile as an indication that there was a depot for wounded men when we heard approaching from an unexpected direction what we know by its whistle was a shell. Dr. MacDonald and I got behind a large gatepost when we heard it strike the ground throwing over us a shower of dirt itself striking the post falling to the ground and rolling around under our feet upon the lower side. We quickly parted company but the shell failed to pursue us with any of its fragments for it did not explode. We regarded this as an intimation to go farther to the rear, and the highest part of the field.

The expectation for this position was grander, except upon the near approach of those shells which the enemy fired for the purpose of destroying or dispersing the wagons then collected. Some of them passed over our heads and others burst in our near vicinity some in the air and some after striking the ground.

During a lull in the firing about noon, Prince moved to another forward position.

I saw our men lying behind temporary protection made with sails and new cut sheaves of wheat when the near whistle of a bullet shot by some rebel sharpshooter made me more cautious. I found Dr. MacDonald who had been with me in the morning behind the post, had established himself in a little hollow with his surgical appliances and attendants and I said to him, that from what I could learn he was in range of a rebel battery which would probably soon open. In a few minutes a shot from a furious attack cut off a horse's nose standing near when the Doctor took my advice and changed his position.

Orders had been given that the medical officers should not occupy a large brick building upon the hill in rear of the battle field on account of the ability of the rebels to shell it, and I went to an unoccupied barn near the river and established a hospital with what supplies I had brought in our retreat and what attendants could be hastily called. When night put an end to the contest our forces held all the ground, they had defended but ours was a traveling army and our wagons having got away, our men, were quietly withdrawn filling the main road down the river with a continuous flow of men and artillery until 9 o' clock next morning.[23]

Fast-moving Confederate forces captured Prince's hospital and more than one hundred wounded Union soldiers. Two days after the Battle of Malvern Hill, on July 3, 1862, Prince and several of his assistants volunteered to accompany the wounded men into captivity in Richmond.

ENDNOTES

[1] Eames, Charles M. *Historic Morgan and Classic Jacksonville. 1884-'85.* The Daily Journal steam job printing office, Jacksonville, IL. 1885. 158.

[2] Donnelley, Lloyd & Company. *History of Morgan County, Illinois: its past and its present.* Chicago. 1878. 438.

[3] *Sangamon Journal/Illinois State Journal.* May 22, 1861. Abraham Lincoln Presidential Library, Springfield, Illinois.

[4] *Collected Works of Abraham Lincoln* Vol. 4. 343.

[5] Adams, George Washington. *Doctors in Blue/The Medical History of the Union Army in the Civil War.* Baton Rouge. Louisiana State University Press. 1952. 15.

[6] Charles A. Tripler to David Prince. *Official Records of the War of Rebellion.* Series1, vol. 5. 79.

[7] Stillé, Charles J. *History of the United States Sanitary Commission.* Philadelphia. J. B. Lippincott & Company. 1866. Chapter II passim.

[8] Stillé, Charles. 58; Adams, George Washington. *Doctors in Blue.* 73.

[9] Perret, Geoffrey. *Lincoln's War.* New York. Random House. 35.

[10] Stillé, Charles. 86-87.

[11] Freemon, Frank R. *Gangrene and Glory.* Madison, N.J. Fairleigh Dickinson University Press. C1998. 222.

[12] Stillé. 266-267.

[13] Stillé. 88-119.

[14] Stillé. 88-119.

[15] Black, Carl E. to Surgeon General of the United States. July 14, 1933. Abraham Lincoln Presidential Library. Carl E. Black Papers. Box 15. "Biographies of Illinois Doctors."

[16] United States Sanitary Commission Medical Archive. Item 511, Reel 4, Frames 0028-0056.

[17] United States Sanitary Commission Medical Archive. Item 511, Reel 4, Frames 0051-0139.

[18] Hamilton, Frank H., M.D. *A Treatise on Military Surgery and Hygiene*. New York. Bailliere Brothers. 1865. 71-73.

[19] Hamilton. 71-73.

[20] Hamilton. 72.

[21] Hamilton. 73-74.

[22] Hamilton. 276.

[23] U. S. Sanitary Commission Medical Archive. Reel 4. Frames 80-87.

VII
Libby Prison and Aftermath

"While the wounded remained near the battle fields, they were under the orders of Gen. Lee and his subordinates, characterized with some of the elements of magnanimity. This could be better appreciated after arriving in Richmond and coming under the tender mercies of Gen. Winder under whose administration of affairs on prisoners we have subsequently had the horrors of Andersonville."

David Prince, "Medical notes of the Peninsular Campaign 1862"

The Battle of Malvern Hill ended July 1, 1862, with Gen. George McClellan's forces retreating to Harrison's Landing on the James River, where they stayed for six weeks until called back to Washington.

David Prince had moved with the army to Harrison's Landing after the Union defeat at Savage's Station on June 29. A small number of the sick and wounded were able to be included in the retreat, but several hundred more were left behind to be captured. Two days after the defeat at Malvern Hill, Prince wrote to Confederate General J.E.B. Stuart, volunteering to be a prisoner with the sick and wounded at Hoxall's Landing.

In the Vicinity of Battlefield of July 1,
Near the James River, Thursday July 3, 1862

Brigadier General Stuart, Commanding C.S. Army

SIR: It is proper for me to state to you that while the U.S. Army was retreating during the night of the first of July, it became known to me that a hospital depot containing over a hundred men too severely wounded to follow the army would be left without any care whatever. I chose to remain with them to do what I could to care for them, and the following enlisted men (most of whom had been connected with the hospital depot before) volunteered to remain with me and throw themselves upon the magnanimity of the government of the Confederate States: [list of Union names and units included].

All but the first three of these and the fifth making four in all were taken from us yesterday as prisoners of war.

We are without food, and if attendants and food are not sent to us, we must starve.

Respectfully yours,

David Prince, Brigade Surgeon, U.S. Volunteer."[1]

Prince wrote about the confusion that enveloped the Union Army after Malvern Hill in his report to the U.S. Sanitary Commission after the war. Prince and two other Army surgeons, Drs. Hammond and Milhaus, had set up a hospital in a two-story house near the James River.

An ambulance load of canned soup, condense milk and other nutrients and appetizers ... were prepared for administration to the men –

exhausted by hardship and hunger as well as the lack of blood and the shock of injuries, but another ambulance filled with rice, sugar, coffee and crackers was turned back in the chaos of the retreat.

It was in the vexation of this disappointment that I saw a long train of ambulances come out from a field near McClellan's headquarters on the river bank and go empty down the road as a part of the grand retreat. For every one of these departing empty ambulances from two to four men went to Richmond who with ordinary management might have been got upon boats and sent north.

Having thus full notice of the retreat of the Army I succeeded by dint of much waiting and perseverance in getting my horse up the road to my hospital. After an hour consultation was had by the medical officers the result of which was many consented to remain with the men and share their fate. After they had gone with the Army and daylight had appeared, I walked over to the house where I had the day before seen Dr. Hammond and Milhaus consulting about the establishment of a hospital. The floors were filled with men having all kinds of wounds, but every medical officer and every nurse had deserted. At first sights there appeared to be but one man with two sound hands and good lower limbs capable of waiting upon the rest and he was a faithful white servant waiting upon a wounded Major who soon *died. As the morning waned however several skulkers came out of their holes and gladly joined the column which continued its retreat down the road, the rear guard remaining until ten o'clock in the morning. For two or three days, however skulkers continued to come out of the woods inquiring for their Regiment, pretending to have had colic or some other equally grave malady.*[2]

Prince and the other physicians sent away all the ambulatory soldiers, which left them with 110 men too severely wounded to walk. That afternoon, however, Stuart's cavalry sent seven of Prince's ten nurses to prison in Richmond.

To Richmond

At this point I went to Richmond. It was as much as the confederates could do to bury the dead and feed the living and carry away their own wounded without stopping for the tender offices of nursing Yankee soldiers.

The journey of the men to Richmond was in Army wagons. They came without straw but as we were at the side of a field of wheat which had just been harvested, we succeeded in getting some of this unthreshed wheat into the wagons. Some of the straw was carried into our prison in Richmond, but its place was never supplied. When this became stale and unfit for use the naked floor was the cleaner resort. It was no little surprise that I looked on and saw the beginning of the packing of this room.

WOUNDED PRISONERS Richmond Dispatch, 7/8/1862

Two hundred wounded Federal soldiers were brought to this city yesterday, in ambulances, from a place called Hoxall's Landing, on James River, and were lodged in the C. S. Hospital. Many of them are wounded desperately, and can hardly hope to recover, while a number have lost either a leg or an arm, and in some individual instances both. Several hundred more, in like condition, will be brought in to-day. The following wounded officers were in the batch that arrived yesterday, viz: S. J. Thompson, Capt. Co. F, 22d Mass.; C. A. Woodworth, Capt. Co. H, 44th N.Y.; C. A. Jones, 2d Lt. Co. E, 1st U.S. Sharpshooters; Chas. Brestele, Capt. Co. C, 7th N.Y. Vols.; Jas. Brown, 2d Lt. Co. A, 62d Penn.; John Pullard, Capt. Co. E, 5th Michigan, Stephen Lang, 2d Lt. Co. E, 7th N. Y. Vols., (leg amputated on the battle-field,) David Prince, Brigade Surgeon U. S. Vols.; Ro. Allen, Jr.; 1st Lt. 1st U. S. Regular Cavalry.

FIGURE 3: Libby Prison, Richmond, Virginia. Gordon Granger. 1865. Library of Congress.

The Confederate government purchased three contiguous warehouses on a canal overlooking the James River from merchant Luther Libby in March 1862 and converted them to a prison. Libby Prison held captured Union officers. Enlisted prisoners were housed in tents on nearby Belle Isle. Conditions were primitive, although Prince credited Confederate administrators with making some efforts toward basic comforts. Prince's first step after arriving at Libby was to clean it up, as best he could.

> *Seizing some stumps of what had been splints made into brooms, and placing them in the hands of my aids or nurses who had been allowed to accompany the train, and calling in aid my old nurses who had been driven off and shut up in the same building, the dirt was partially removed from the place the next man was to occupy, before he got there.*

> *This was a hospital – Hospital No 4. I inquired of the lieutenant of the guard how soon rations would be forwarded to the men. 'Have you made your requisition?' said he. This astonished me that under the authority of the confederacy I should be expected to make requisition for everything these men could get: except water. Let the rebels in Richmond be praised, even though the soul of Gen. Winder should get a share, for having introduced a liberal supply of water into all the Richmond prisons. This came from the James River some miles above, through the general supply for the City.*

This water kept off erysipelas and gangrene affording the means of rinsing the dressing to any extent though if contagion has one got into them, we had no boiling water with which to destroy it presence in the dressing, which could be thrown away. The appliances of my 'Hospital' was a floor upon to lie and lucky was the man who had a blanket of his own, else went without: a water cock in one end of the room flowing into a trough then exit pipe from which could be plugged so as to connect it with a wash tub, a sink in the basement to which those who could walk could go, and a hospital knapsack and its contents which we carried with us. But there were urgent necessities of urination and defecation. Some old bottles and pans used for this purpose in the field hospital had been left behind under the supposition that in a Richmond Hospital, similar appliances would be furnished.

I obtained from the lieutenant of the guard permission to go out into the city to see if I could buy some of these indispensables. After searching a long distance (accompanied by a confederate soldier walking behind me with a musket) I succeeded in purchasing three or four bottles for usuals and a couple of stoneware pans, in place of the regular appliances.

The theoretic daily ration for the men was a pound of bread and a pound of meat supplied in two meals, the work of the cooking and

Robert Berry

distribution being done by union prisoners. This was of a good quality generally.

Later in this prison hospital some opium combined with other medicine were obtained from the medical supply in the Hospital in the Libby prison proper, and later our nurses were packed up and carried to a much less comfortable place without any apparent reason, and with none assigned. This of course made a new combination of patients, taking from new ones that I had taken an interest in and giving me many others that I had never seen before, breaking up all systems by which each nurse was held responsible for his men, and producing general confusion and discouragement.

It might as well be somewhere said for the benefit of those who have no other means of knowing that camp lice delighting in the seat-perfume of long worn garments are very little disturbed by cold water bathing. They are quiet for a while but as soon as the water has the time to dry off, they are as nimble as ever.

Living among the seams and other hiding places of the clothing and only going upon the persons for meals for which that have as is now the custom for oil and salt, and multiplying with wonderful rapidity in their fastnesses. Benzenes would probably be effective as it is to other parasites but they are not known to have been tried in Richmond.

A prisoner deprived of the use of hot water soon learns to appreciate the anti-lice performance of picking. Grounded upon their native leaning against the wall or a post, the whole congregation may be seen two or three times a day, with heads depressed like catholic devotees counting their beads, only that instead of beads rapidly fingered from one portion of a string to another, the rapid succession of audible snaps, indicates the destruction of life by the method of squeezing between two thumb nails. Continued picking keeps down the increase but the parasites are on the floor, walls and ceiling in their peregrinations in search of a better pasturage and they thus make their approach from every direction.

Woe be to the sick man whose energy is insufficient for the divine exercise of extermination, for though half dead, he soon becomes alive with new phenomena of motion, reaching up his garments gray with a new life drawn from his own blood. Prisoners who were ill, as opposed to wounded, suffered most.

It was horrible to see in these sad fights some of the men for whom their medical officers had in vain sought the privilege of sending them to the rear before the seven days fighting. ... Poor creatures, had they been struck with bombs or bullets instead of dysentery and fever, they might have gone to the hospitable shores of the North instead of the lice dens of Richmond.[3]

Prince spent twenty-four days in Confederate custody, including nineteen days at Libby Prison. He and twenty-two other Union surgeons and assistant surgeons were exchanged for about seventy Confederate physicians. The exchange agreement required that released prisoners not return to the battlefield, so Prince resigned from the Union Army on September 22, 1862.

> *"Dr. Prince – We learn with great pleasure that Dr. Prince, who was taken prisoner at Richmond, has been released and is again at his post of duty. The report that he was wounded is incorrect."*
> *Jacksonville Journal,* August 2, 1862

> *"Dr. Prince. This gentleman who has been in the service since the commencement of the war as Surgeon, and for a time prisoner in Virginia, we learn, has resigned and is once more enjoying the privileges of civil life in our midst."*
> *Jacksonville Journal,* October 30, 1862

Prince Returns Home

David Prince returned to Jacksonville in October 1862 and quickly re-established his medical practice. He published his card in the November 5, 1862 issue of the *Jacksonville Journal.* In addition to his regular medical duties, Prince served as an Illinois draft board surgeon from May 1 to August 1, 1863 (the military draft in Illinois ended in September 1863).[4] He also began to refine his thoughts about ways doctors could have provided better care to their military patients, focusing on the importance of proper ventilation.

When the war ended in 1865, the U.S. Sanitary Commission invited medical men in each state to provide material for publication of *Hygienic Medical and Surgical History of the War*. From September to December 1865, Prince was hired for ten dollars a day to recruit contributions from doctors in Pennsylvania, West Virginia, and Maryland. Also, as part of the medical history, Prince prepared reports on his experiences in the war based on notes in his personal diary. Much of his report involved his role with the Army of the Potomac, published under the title "Medical Notes of the Peninsula Campaign." The complete text is included in the twenty-five volumes of *Surgical Memoirs War of the Rebellion, Collected and Published by the United States Sanitary Commission* (1871).

Prince's essays covered subjects ranging from skull injuries to foot amputations, sometimes including brief descriptions of other physicians' unique methods. His reports contained minute details of many topics, none more comprehensive than an essay on "Posture Dressings and the Daily Care of Wounded Parts." "This subject must be one of the most important in Surgery and most worthy of full elucidation, especially in the relations, as it involves the form and principles of what is to be done every day and every hour to save life and to avoid deformity," he wrote. The material from many of these reports was later published in medical journals. In addition to the Peninsula Campaign reports, Prince submitted other documents describing battlefield surgical procedures performed by him and others.

Early in 1865, Prince corresponded with Dr. John Snyder, who had recently settled in Virginia, Illinois. Their letters discussed patient cases and sharing of medical books. Snyder (1865-1921) was born in Belleville, Illinois and graduated from MacDonald's Medical School in St. Louis in 1853. While starting a practice in Illinois, he also was involved in Democratic state politics (a topic of interest to Prince). During the Civil War, Snyder served as a line officer with Confederate forces from southern Missouri. After the war, Snyder returned to Illinois to find a place to establish a practice. Petitioners in Virginia wished to have him "because the only good doctor in Virginia was Republican." As a member of the Illinois legislature in 1878, Snyder supported the creation of the Illinois Historical Library. He also helped establish the Illinois State Historical Society and served as its third president in 1903.[5]

In a June 25, 1865 letter to Snyder, Prince shared a personal note: "I am going to be absent from Jacksonville for a while and perhaps permanently. I am soon going with the employment of the Sanitary Commission in making up its statistics and other information of a hygienic and medical character with reference to publication. It is probable that I shall change my place of residence when I am through with that work."[6]

In his travels for the USSC, Prince kept in regular contact with Dr. Elisha Harris, secretary of the Sanitary Commission, through registered mail and occasional trips to the New York office. Sanitary Commission records show Prince sent Harris nineteen letters and seven essays. Prince was provided with a list of doctors and their locations. In addition to interviewing doctors, Prince distributed a circular that noted the information would be collected and revised in order not to interfere with the history being prepared by the Medical Bureau of Washington. The circular listed four areas of interest: I. Organization and character of volunteer forces in battle. II. Military hygiene and camp diseases in the field, hospitals, and naval vessels. III. Surgery of the war. IV. hospitals, ambulances, water transportation and battle field succor, with the history of improvements in methods and appliances.[7]

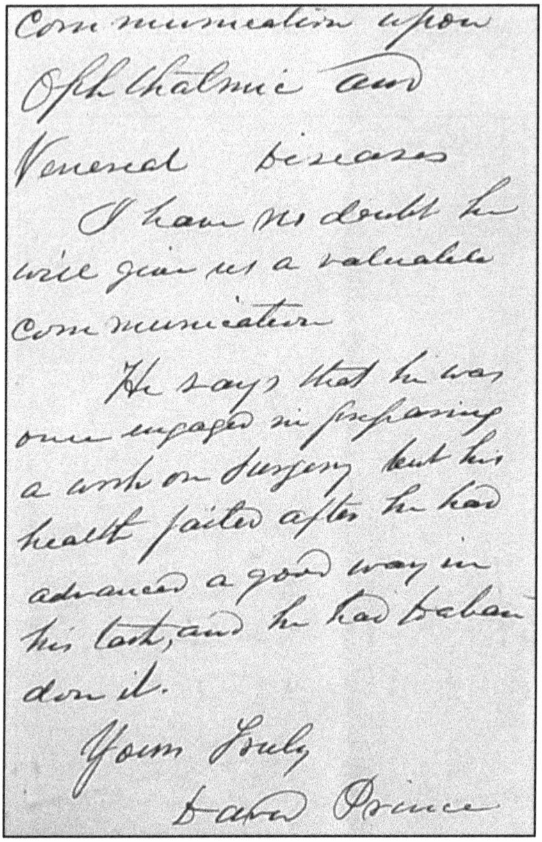

Communication upon
Ophthalmic and
Venereal diseases
I have no doubt he
will give us a valuable
communication
He says that he was
once engaged in preparing
a work on Surgery but his
health failed after he had
advanced a good way in
his task, and he had to abandon
it.
Yours Truly
David Prince

FIGURE 4: David Prince to Elisha Harris. September 24, 1865.

More than once, Prince requested additional circulars in packages to be picked up at USSC offices in hospitals, among them two hundred for Philadelphia and sixty to one hundred he anticipated needing for Maryland. Letters Prince sent to Harris indicated "there is much interest in our enterprise." His encounters with doctors varied greatly. He described one doctor as "considerably talented," but also "indolently inclined." The physician told Prince he did not keep notes. Another, however, had done extensive medical writing and told Prince he might submit as many as two hundred papers about surgery that was "carefully observed." In Harrisburg, a doctor suggested Prince contact Dr. Cresson Stiles at Kisip Hospital in Long Island, who was described as "a careful observer and a good writer." At least one doctor inquired about compensation and was referred to Harris for an answer.[8]

In his travels for the Sanitary Commission, Prince had long train rides with time to reflect on his personal experiences. One issue on his mind was the unhealthy conditions he reported on in Washington, D.C. in January 1862. Prince noted the contribution of overcrowding and lack of ventilation to high rates of sickness among Union soldiers. The incidents he saw in Washington and throughout the Peninsula Campaign contributed to Prince's later preoccupation with the importance of air quality and ventilation to his patients' chances for recuperation.

Prince wrote an out-of-the-ordinary letter to Harris during a long wait for a connection at the junction of the Northern Central and Gettysburg Railroad in Pennsylvania on September 28, 1865. The letter included a drawing of a patient on a bed with a crude ventilating system; Prince called it a "homely picture" of a sleeping patient.

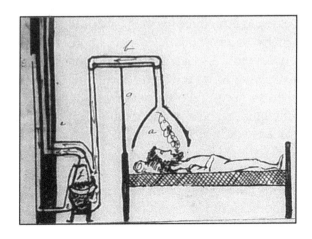

*FIGURE 5: Ventilator drawing in David Prince
to Elisha Harris. September 28, 1865.*

His description lists: "a) a funnel receiving the expired air; b) Tube leading off supported by the rest; c) Flue carrying away so much of the vitiated air as back to enter stove; d) smoke pipe represented alongside of the other but better enclosed by the vitiated air flue; e) Entrance of outdoor air which is more pure if brought from a height from the ground to be free from emanations; f) a common stove covered in front by an apron which obliges it to receive its air for combustion from the tubes to carrying vitiated air. This enters the vent below as well as the opening above the flames when opened to moderate the heat. The remainder of this vitiated air goes up the tube c. (What is represented here as being done for one room may be done for a whole house by conducting tubes to the furnace in the basement. While fires are kept up, this is the most practical method, it would seem, but with fires in the warm weather an exhaust fan moved by machinery amount to the most reliable.)"[9]

Up to the 1860s, conventional wisdom held that sickness and fevers were attributable to malaria (colloquial Italian for "bad air") or miasma (noxious air from rotting vegetation). Generally, the question of how infection endured in dwellings, hospitals, and other overcrowded places puzzled physicians in the early nineteenth century, prior to the development of bacteriology and virology. This mystery was solved in the second half of the century by the research of Louis Pasteur in microbiology, followed by Joseph Lister in antiseptic surgery.

For Prince, ventilation was a key piece of the hygiene puzzle. In an 1866 article for the *Chicago Medical Examiner,* he reported: "Upon the subject of ventilation, the problem has been how to secure the comfort of a home with the purity of outdoor air. It has been supposed that this was the utmost possible attainment. More than this has been achieved. It has been found practicable to make an artificial mountain air without its rarity.

"Mr. A.S. Lyman has, through twenty years of study and experiment, finally perfected an arrangement of chemical agents, so as to deprive the air of all its impurities and make it equal to that found above the influence of emanations from the surface of the earth." Among the first beds with the purifying attachment were those operated at Bellevue Hospital "to the very great satisfaction of those who have watched the progress of the cases submitted to the influence of the purified air," Prince wrote.[10]

Azel Storrs Lyman (1815-1885), an inventor in New York City, patented an air purifier for ventilating beds, desks, and rooms of all sizes in 1865. (Lyman also was one of the first to invent a fountain pen, holder and nib (1848); later he invented a steam boiler alarm, an air pump and an improved metal can for preserving food.)

The process, Prince wrote, begins "by passing air over unslaked lime, which absorbs carbonic acid and some water and organic impurities, and elevates its temperature, giving it a tendency to rise. It then passes through fresh-burned charcoal, losing most of the impurities which the lime had not taken up. The purified air then ascends to the top of the apparatus, and, turning to descend, it passes over ice, which cools it and accelerates the current, which next passes out through orifices in which the current is divided up by wire screens, so as not to blow in one compact current."[11]

FIGURE 6: Illustrations from Prince's "Lyman's Air Purifier."

When the war and his work for the Sanitary Commission ended, Prince focused on rebuilding his medical practice in Jacksonville, contributing to medical journals, and re-establishing the Morgan County Medical Society. In 1867, Prince applied his understanding of ventilation and air purification to the operation of his own sanitarium.

ENDNOTES

[1] David Prince to Gen. J.E.B. Stuart. July 3, 1862. Official Records, Series II, Vol. 4. 118.

[2] United States Sanitary Commission Medical Archive. Item 511, Reel 4, Frames 0126-0144.

[3] U.S. Sanitary Commission. Film records. Reel 5, Frames 1031-1099. New York Public Library.

[4] "No Draft in Illinois." *Jacksonville Journal*. October, 1863.

[5] Pearson, Emmet F. "A Pioneer Illinois Physician and Scholar: John F. Snyder, MD" *Illinois Medical Journal*. November 1988. Vol. 174:5. Passim.

[6] Prince to John Snyder. June 25, 1865. Abraham Lincoln Presidential Library. Dr. John F. Snyder Papers. Box 4, Correspondence.

[7] USSC Film Records. Reel 2, Frame 0945.

[8] USSC Film Records. Reel 5, Frame 0851.

[9] USSC Film Records. Reel 2, Frame 0962; Prince to Elisha Harris. September 28, 1865. USSC Film records. Reel 2. Frame 0962.

[10] Prince. "Lyman's Air Purifier." *Chicago Medical Examiner*. February 1866. Edited by N. S. Davis, M.D.

[11] Prince. "Lyman's Air Purifier".

VIII
The Ventilated Sanitarium

"It was not until his return to Jacksonville after the War that the most active years of Prince's life began. In 1867, he bought a large house on Sandy Street and established for himself a private hospital for the care of surgical cases and chronic diseases. This intimate contact with a sanitarium of his own must have stimulated him in his work for, from this time on, his writing was prolific."
Carl E. Black, M.D., "Biography
of Illinois Doctors," unpublished.

David Prince sought to broaden his medical practice in 1867 by establishing the first infirmary in Jacksonville, a building later named the David Prince Sanitarium. He contracted with Judge William Thomas on July 13, 1867 to buy a four-story building on South Sandy Street, just off the southwest corner of the village square. The price was twelve thousand dollars – four thousand dollars when the contract was signed and the remainder due under the terms of a vendor lien paid off in four years.[1]

Remodeling began shortly after the down payment was made. Prince's goal was to have a facility that would provide professional nursing and everyday care for patients who required it. The facility eventually could accommodate about twenty patients. There were rooms for patients, an office, a kitchen, a dissection room and a surgery room. Initially, the surgery room included Lister's invention for antiseptic surgery, which sprayed a diluted carbolic acid cloud over the patient and surgeon. The hand pump was operated by assistant.

In a November 20, 1867 letter to Dr. John Snyder, Prince gave Snyder detailed instructions for treating a patient of Snyder's who had a uterine problem. He then launched into a description of the infirmary: "I am getting my Infirmary nearly ready for occupation and shall be very glad to have you come and inspect it. I am introducing a feature which is nearly new in hospitals. Indeed, I do not know that it has been introduced into any institution. I have the building heated by furnaces and the cold air to be heated by these first passed through fresh coke or charcoal, then over lime, then into the furnace chamber and then throughout the house. I thus have not only ventilation, but better, the introduction of a purified air into all the house changing the climate on a small scale, that is, to the extent of the rooms thus warmed. I think I shall make a climate which will make a good winter retreat for consumptives."[2]

A few weeks after this letter, the editor of the *Jacksonville Weekly Journal* described the work under way:

> *"Passing down Sandy Street yesterday, we observed the carpenters at work on the Infirmary, being fitted up by Dr. Prince, and not having previously examined its internal arrangements, we embraced the occasion to pass through the entire building. We found the doctor, earnestly engaged directing and superintending every department, and we are glad to say that our citizens cannot fail to feel great pride in the admirable plans and neat arrangements of the building. We are proud of all our institutions, our Blind, Insane, Deaf and Dumb, Idiotic, our schools and colleges, and we may now add our*

Infirmary, for in ten days this will take its place as one, but by no means the least, of the institutions of our city. No city of the size and pretentions of ours, should be without a general hospital, and much credit is due Dr. Prince for his enterprise in establishing this Infirmary. We were much delighted with the novel arrangements the doctor has just completed for purifying the air; an arrangement by which all the air that is used for healing purposes first passes through recently-burned coke, placed upon shelves, and then enters the furnace chambers to be heated for distribution through the house. By this arrangement, motes and chemical impurities are arrested, giving the air the purity of mountain regions."[3]

THE PRINCE SANITARIUM, JACKSONVILLE, ILLINOIS

Figure 7: David Prince Sanitarium, South Sandy Street, Jacksonville, IL 1867-1890.

Eight months after remodeling began, Snyder inquired about the progress of the infirmary. Prince responded in a letter dated April 4, 1868: "Well the house is at this moment full. It may not be full next week, but it is more likely to be than not to be. I did not miscalculate regarding the enterprise. Its success puts it beyond the condition of an experiment."[4]

A more elaborately antiseptic surgical theater was added over the next decade. Prince continued to work on improvements and on constructing a fully antiseptic operating room. He made some final additions in 1884 and 1885 after visiting the offices of Pasteur and Lister while attending medical conferences in Paris and London.

Prince's antiseptic surgical theater was in a separate two-story building six feet from the main building, accessed by an outside platform. The purification system for the operating room was in the basement, separated by seven layers from the operating room above. Air was sprayed with steam when entering. On the basement ceiling, heated paraffin filled the joist cracks. The ceiling was covered by tarred paper, painted, covered with muslin, and painted again. The yellow pine floor of the operating room was also sealed with paraffin driven as deeply as possible into the floor by a warmed iron. All the woodwork was painted or paraffined. When needed, frames with muslin tacked to them could be set up against open windows away from the wind, with the upper sash pulled down to hold the frame.[5]

Air from the outside was treated with three filtrations beginning at a twenty-inch ventilator with a steam jet and continuing through two artificial showers and screens, eventually being warmed by a stove before entering the operating room. "It is supposed that enough air will enter and escape to change the whole volume of the air once in fifteen minutes," according to Prince.

Lister's antiseptic surgery practices included personal preparation by the surgeon. For Prince, "useful precautions" included a bath, dampening the hair, clean clothing, wearing a gown, and cleaning hands with a nail brush and a solution of "carbonic acid, mercuric bichloride, or permanganate of potash." Prince continued use of the Lister spray pump during surgery.[6]

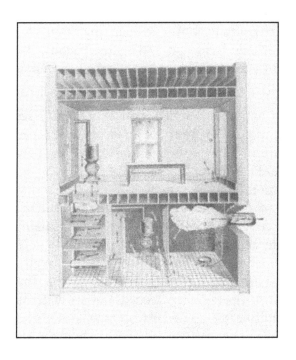

Figure 8: Operating room with purified air. David Prince. "A Devise for Atmospheric Purification." 1885.

Prince regularly took on assistants who were preparing for medical school, he added more when the sanitarium was in operation. Summer intern Thomas Hall Shastid was preparing for entrance to Northwestern University Medical School in 1874. "It became almost a rage throughout the Upper Mississippi Valley for doctors to send (Prince) all the cleft-palate cases they could find. I once assisted in the performance of five cleft-palate operations in one single day.

"But Prince was a good all-around surgeon too. He operated for cross-eyes and cataracts literally by the hundreds. (Incidentally, in my early boyhood, he operated on my grandfather, Thomas Hall, for two cataracts on the same day, and both of them quite successfully.) He was, indeed, quite swiftly becoming more widely known as an oculistic than as an orthopedic and general surgeon."[7]

Carl Black was a student of Prince in 1884 and 1885. Black's diary of his time at the Prince Sanitarium begins with his studying *Gray's Anatomy* and Kirk's *Physiology*. After a month, Black commented, "studying a little dull." However, he also was greatly interested in witnessing several difficult abdominal operations performed by Prince and cataract surgeries by Prince's son, Dr. Arthur Prince, who specialized in eye diseases. Dissection lessons began with animals, such as the removal of the kidney of a dog. But this was a decade after Illinois law provided a legal means for obtaining human bodies to dissect, and students were anxious to begin lessons in dissection of human cadavers. In February 1885, Black's diary noted, "Prince never passed a winter without a stiff."[8]

In 1884, the local newspaper reported that the sanitarium was treating three thousand patients a year. Dr. Arthur Edward Prince joined his father's practice at the sanitarium in 1878, taking over patients who needed treatment for eye, ear, nose, and throat disorders. He had graduated from the College of Physicians and Surgeons in New York City, then went to Europe for special studies of eye and ear diseases at Vienna University. Dr. John Abbot Prince, the younger son, joined his father's practice in 1887 as a general surgeon after graduating from the University of Michigan Medical School.[9]

Once the sanitarium was well established, David Prince published a broadside to promote the enterprise:[10]

SANITARIUM.

This is an establishment in which provision is made for the rational application of the principal appliances employed in the treatment by friction, kneading and passive motion; by water and heat, and by electricity.

These agents are employed in combination or alteration, with a careful scrutiny in regard to the requirements of each particular case. It cannot be said of them that "If they do no good they can do no harm,"

Chronic inflammations and nervous derangements are found to yield to these agencies in some cases in which medicine alone is inadequate.

Deformities and debilities are treated by surgical operations and mechanical appliances when necessary, and also by bathing, friction movements and electrical excitation.

It is a home for persons undergoing surgical treatment, enabling them to be constantly under the supervision of skilled attendants.

It is intended that this enterprise shall be in the future, as in the past, so conducted as to secure the confidence of the medical profession.

Among the Appliances of this Establishment Are:

1. Air pumps and vacuum boots for atmospheric exhaustion after the plan of Junod.

2. A galvanic battery of 220 cells, of the specific gravity style, the elements being zinc and copper—the zinc above, surrounded by a solution of sulphate of zinc, and the copper below, surrounded by a solution of sulphate of copper. The current from this battery is employed for the dispersion of tumors and growths of plastic deposits—for the correction of perversions of innervation, and for the removal of lumbago and other forms of muscular rheumatism. When the current is interrupted by a vibrator in rapid motion, the resolving effects are combined with the stimulating effects upon the muscular fibres which are commonly secured by the faradic or induction current, which latter current is produced by small and less expensive apparatus which can be carried about.

3. A soapstone bath tub with electrodes for the most effectual employment of both the galvanic and the faradics current, in connection with warm water. This is the most agreeable, and, for some diseases, the most useful mode in which electricity can be employed.

4. A machine of new construction for friction, kneading and vibration, processes included in the newly introduced word, *massage*. The fatigue attending the application of these agents by hand is a bar to their faithful and effectual employment. Acute inflammation contraindicates *massage* and electrization, while bathing is applicable to this condition. Congestion and the chronic sequels of inflammation are benefited by the last three of these appliances, while the first is especially applicable to wasting or emaciation, accompanied by coldness from arterial contraction.

DAVID PRINCE, M. D.,
JACKSONVILLE, ILL.   **Proprietor.**

Figure 9: Prince Sanitarium broadside.
Abraham Lincoln Presidential Library.

ENDNOTES

[1] Recorder of Deeds. Morgan County Clerk. Morgan County, Illinois.

[2] David Prince to John Snyder. November 20, 1867. Abraham Lincoln Presidential Library. Snyder Papers, Box 4. Correspondence.

[3] "City News." *Jacksonville Weekly Journal.* December 5, 1867.

[4] Prince to Snyder. April 4, 1868. Abraham Lincoln Presidential Library. Snyder Papers, Box 4. Correspondence.

[5] Prince, David, M.D. "A Devise for Atmospheric Purification." *Transactions of the American Surgical Association.* Volume Three. Philadelphia. P. Blackiston, Sons & Company. 1885. 391.

[6] Prince. "A Devise for Atmospheric Purification. Transactions of the American Surgical Association. Vol. 3. 1885." 391-392.

[7] Shastid, Thomas Hall. *My Second Life.* 565.

[8] Black, Carl E., M.D. "Diaries" (1884 - 1885). Carl E. Black Papers. Abraham Lincoln Presidential Library. Springfield, Illinois. Box 6, Folder 9. Daily activities for period of studying medicine under preceptor David Prince at sanitarium from October 21, 1884 to June 1885.

[9] Norbury, Frank B. M.D. "David Prince: Pioneer Surgeon". *Illinois Medical Journal.* May 1966.

[10] Prince, David, M.D. Broadside for Sanitarium. Abraham Lincoln Presidential Library, Manuscripts. B-1492.

IX
Medical Publications

"Prince's many publications testify to his prodigious reading and activity; his medical society activities and his correspondence underscore broad concern with improving medicine."
John K. Crellin, Medical Care in Pioneer Illinois

David Prince prefaces his 1873 book, *Galvano-Therapeutics,* by saying he hopes "to contribute something to the general fund of information, in exchange for what he (Prince) is constantly deriving from other laborers in the same field. This essay is thus to be regarded as of temporary utility, like the clover which the farmer turns under, in order to enrich his field for the production of a final crop, which once in the granary, will have an element of permanence." Readers should not consider his reports to be textbooks, Prince adds, because that would "embarrass the introduction of new and better views."[1]

The extent to which Prince sought medical information from others is evident by his large personal library, which included European material; he read German and French medical literature. His writings always gave credit to the work and opinions of others, both those with which he agreed and those he did not. Carl E. Black prepared a bibliography of Prince's 122 works -- books, journals, monographs, lectures, and personal letters. Black found 184 quotes and 569 references to other surgeons in addition to citations for 223 illustrations.[2]

Prince had been writing articles for medical journals since the early 1840s. He published his first book in 1866: *Orthopedics: A Systematic Treatise upon the Prevention and Correction of Deformities*. Two years later, he published his second book, *Plastics: A New Classification and a Brief Exposition of Plastic Surgery*. These two books were later reprinted as a single volume in 1871. Subsequent republications of the combined volume were bound with other reports by Prince.

The intended audience for *Orthopedics* was general practice physicians outside large cities whose patients need attention for deformities, diseases, or accidents. Prince explained his goal in writing *Orthopedics*: "In order to render the advance in knowledge on this subject, gained with the last twenty years, accessible to the mass of the profession it is necessary that the substance of many valuable essays and monographs should be sifted and collected into a few pages, with the means of all to purchase it and with the time of all to read it. To these ends, an attempt has been made to connect the medical treatment with the mechanical, in order to give the work its nearest practical approach to completeness, compatible with the necessary brevity."[3]

Orthopedics discusses many of the deformities, their causes and cures, in clinical detail, including consideration of muscles, tendons, and blood vessels. Prince devoted extensive attention to the congenital deformities of cleft palate, clubfoot, spinal curvature and spina bifida. He described the history of attempts to reconstruct cleft palates, noting that the firmness of bones made it difficult to close the bony arch. In the early 1800s, surgeons achieved limited success by applying unvulcanized rubber. American surgeon Norman W. Kingsley of New York constructed an artificial palate of molded vulcanized soft rubber in 1859. The artificial palate improved speech and articulation within weeks. This was demonstrated at the 1864 meeting of the American Medical Association by one of Kingsley's patients.[4]

The Philadelphia publisher of *Orthopedics*, Lindsay and Blakiston, solicited comments from the profession to write a review that would appear in the front piece of Prince's 1866 book on plastic surgery. Dr. Samuel Gross wrote:

> *"Gentlemen:*
> *"I thank you for the copy of Dr. Prince's Orthopedics. The work is an excellent resume of the existing state of the art and science of which it treats, and will, I doubt not, meet with universal favor of the profession. The manner in which the treatise is gotten up, reflects credit upon your house. I am, gentlemen,*
> *"Very respectfully, your friend,*
> *"S. D. Gross."[5]*

Prince continued work on cleft palate advancements into the 1870s in collaboration with Jacksonville dentist Greene Vardiman Black. They sought a surgical solution, which was achieved after Black's invention of a pickup needle that received international recognition in the 1880s. Prince's skill, especially for treating cleft palate and club foot, became so widely known that area physicians referred patients to Prince, and he was sought out by patients' families from neighboring states.

For deformities caused by accidents or inflammation, treatments involved splints or braces of varying complexity. Prince's discussion of treating hip, knee diseases and deformities included elaborate apparatus extensions invented by physicians in Chicago, New York, Philadelphia and Europe. These were often beyond the skill of a local blacksmith or carpenter, the artisans most often available to general practitioners outside cities. Alternatively, Prince offered a form for a simple brace he settled on after several trials. It had a wood shaft with an iron pelvic collar at the top and an iron foot-rod extending beyond the foot to pass through the heel of a shoe.[6]

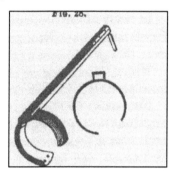

Figure 10: Prince's Ischiatic crutch for extension in diseases of the hip and knee joints. The small figure is a profile of the collar attached to the end of the staff.[7]

Prince, however, had an advantage over most physicians practicing outside cities. In 1865, E. R. Sieber moved to Jacksonville from Tennessee to open a hardware store where he made Kentucky rifles, pistols and barbed wire fences. Sieber had previously been an inspector for the Union army in the Civil War. Prince engaged Sieber to make braces for him.[8]

Prince concluded an overview of five classifications of deformities with an historical reference to "fashionable" intentional mutilation, such as the ancient practice of Chinese grandees compressing the feet of female children. To a lesser degree, he pointed to the feet and waists of genteelly educated children in modern American and European society. Prince noted what he called the "folly" of mothers who had their daughters wear fashionable shoes too narrow for the feet and clothing with narrow waists: "Not the least deplorable condition of the deformities resulting from these usages is the impossibility of removing in the adult the misshapes acquired in childhood and youth. A deformity, admitted to be such, may be subjected to treatment early; but a deformity, deemed fashionable, will receive no attempt at remedy, until suffering prompts the victim, too late, to seek relief."[9]

Several medical journals offered favorable reviews following publication of Prince's *Orthopedics.* "Prepared with especial reference to the wants of the general practitioner, it is intended for a well-digested outline of all that is known of the cause, prevention and cure of a very interesting and but little understood class of diseases," the *New York Medical Record* said. "His descriptions are clear and concise. His views are tenable and his deductions are eminently practical."[10]

Prince differentiated orthopedics and plastic surgery in the introduction to his second book; *Plastics: A New Classification and a Brief Exposition of Plastic Surgery.* In orthopedic surgery, he wrote, the process of correcting deformities involves methods that are attained "chiefly by mechanism, posture, and exercise, and by such cutting processes as come to the aid of mechanism and posture, causing parts to yield more rapidly than can be effected by mere force directly applied, and thus enabling the surgeon to save time." Plastic surgery, he says, involves "cutting or tearing, and by exudations, adhesions and granulations which follow." Plastic surgery as a scientific conception was no older than the nineteenth century, according to Prince. "It is even now in its infancy and is to grow into maturity by a better knowledge of general and local therapeutics applicable to the healing of wounds and to better conceptions of mechanical execution."[11]

Plastics was published in 1868, two years after *Orthopedics,* and contains many references to medical journal articles published the same year. Prince focused on surgeries to the face, with lesser attention to plastic surgeries of the genitals and the bladder. The methods described involve grafting and transplanting, as well as cutting and handling flaps to provide nutrition and arterial health in resupplying blood to the flaps after removal of deformities.

Dr. Frank B. Norbury of Jacksonville wrote a century later that "David Prince was performing surgical procedures in the last century which are not even done in Jacksonville today (1980), and not done in Springfield until the arrival on the scene of modern plastic surgeons in the 1970s."[12]

Prince's third book, *Galvano-Therapeutics A Revised Reprint*, a report published in 1874 made to the Illinois State Medical Society, discussed his experimentation with therapies using electrical current. Bathing with electric eels was considered therapeutic in ancient times. It was not until the late eighteenth century that Italian scientist Luigi Galvani pioneered electrophysiology, the effects of electricity on animal tissue. Forty years later, English scientist Michael Faraday discovered the principles of electromagnetic induction, diamagnetism and electrolysis.

In most therapeutic cases, Prince applied Galvani's current in a closed circuit and Faraday's induction less often. "The faradic apparatus is cheap, light and easily transportable, and its effects upon the nerves of sensation are very marked," Prince wrote, while "the galvanic current flows without noise and sensation, except in large current, and acts catalytically, and upon a different class of affections from those which are most benefited by faradic current." The size and maintenance of cell batteries made their medical use impractical in the first half of the nineteenth century. However, smaller, more utilitarian cell batteries came with the invention of the telegraph by Samuel Morse in the 1830s and 1840s. In the next two decades, surgeons in America and Europe began to apply electrical therapeutic methods, often experimentally and with mixed results.[13]

"Notwithstanding the fact established by Humboldt in the later years of the last century, that the galvanic current has great power over the secretions and its previously known power over nervous sensibility and muscular contraction, the knowledge of its therapeutic applications has exhibited a slow and fitful growth," Prince wrote in *Galvano-Therapeutics*. "So much extravagance has from time to time been mixed, as chaff with the few grains of truth, that routine practitioners have turned with disgust from the whole subject." When Prince recommended galvanic current to "a very scientific old gentleman" who came to him complaining of chronic lameness: "He replied, that he believed that all intelligent medical men had discarded the use of electricity as a humbug."[14]

Many surgeons published their methodologies in journals, openly reporting failures when they occurred. It developed that the crucial element in applying electricity in surgeries was controlling the galvanic current; too low resulted in no effect, too high resulted in pain or death. Prince referenced the reports of twenty-seven surgeons, European and American. He commented at length on the reports that were helpful to him. Those he dismissed either contained errors or, in his opinion, demonstrated a lack of scientific knowledge or skill.

Prince followed journal articles on the use of electricity until he was able to construct space for electrotherapy in his sanitarium a decade after its opening. He purchased a battery containing 120 cells from the Galvano-Faradic Manufacturing Company of New York. In addition, he purchased a regulator for controlling current.[15]

Figure 11: *"Three cells in position, showing the relations of the electro-motor elements, and their connection from cell to cell. The heavier shading represents the blue sulphate of copper, and light shading, the while sulphate of zinc."* Galvano-Therapeutics.

Figure 12: "Bartlett's Regulator, arranged for 60 cells, with current selectors, a current reverser, and Powell's clock-work interrupter." Galvano-Therapeutics.

Many applications of galvanic procedures provide nutrients to muscles and nerves. The electric charge causes the muscles to contract after which relaxation lets blood return to the muscles thus restoring nutrients. "The applications were each day varied, in an experimental search for the best method," Prince wrote. Each case was unique in the number of cells employed and the length of time applied; some began with ten cells for ten minutes and increased over a period of days with interruption periods varying from ten minutes to two hours, depending on the patient's endurance. Overall, treatments varied from a few days to a month or more. Prince found that even procedures that weren't completely successful did provide some relief from chronic pain. He also found that galvanic current was not useful when inflammation was present because it increased heat to the area. Some treatments were easy. In one case, a well-digger sprained his small finger severely enough to prevent him from holding a shovel or pick. "One application of the current greatly benefited the finger, and a few applications more made the finger fit to handle of the pick without pain."[16]

The treatment often reduced pain and stiffness, Prince found. Prince treated a sixty-year-old woman who referred to her condition as rheumatism. In her first treatment, Prince applied the full strength of one hundred twenty cells for seven sittings of half an hour each. Afterwards, she was much improved: "She required to ride, now she walks," Prince wrote. Ten days later: "She has had six more sittings, with great improvement, not only with pain and lameness, but in all her functions. No medicine has been prescribed. This case is a sample of numerous cases of pain and stiffness not well defined, capable of being relieved by a strong continuous galvanic current."[17]

Prince likewise described success in other types of cases, including neuralgia, general prostration, sprains and bed sores. He also was able to remove some growths on the skin, such as warts, via galvanic cauterization. A platinum wire was preferred, because it warmed quickly and at higher temperatures did not burst into flames, as did iron wire. The platinum wire passed through a wood handle and looped. The loop pulled tight against the wart's base severed the growth and cauterized the wound.

However, Prince found that galvanic therapies weren't any better than other remedies for eczema and psoriasis. "The determination of the real value of the remedy requires more experience," he wrote. The value of galvanism in treating skin diseases, Prince wrote, "is still in the experimental period. Enough is known, however, to warrant the expectation, that this agent will prove of more value than any other, in the removal of non-contagious affections of the skin."[18]

Prince briefly discussed electric bath therapy. "As the salts of the body make a better conductor than water, it is very easy to convey the current, whether galvanic or faradic, through the body, surrounded by water." Two large sponges were dropped in the water, one attached to the copper end of the battery, the other to the zinc end. For electric baths, some physicians used bathtubs of painted wood or lined tubs with strong rubber cloth, as in diving bells. Prince installed a soapstone bathtub in his sanitarium. "The faradic bath is exhilarating, and, if only continued for a few minutes, it is safe."[19]

Small vascular tumors were treated successfully with electrolysis. Large non-cancerous tumors were also treated successfully by being dissected with a knife, requiring healing of the wound, before galvanization was applied. A forty-year-old man presented a tumor under the right jaw that had been growing for two years. The tumor was first dissected from the underside. A week later, galvanization commenced, using a 32-cell battery for an average of twenty minutes twice a day. After a month, a new growth appeared under the ear. No attempt was made to remove all of it. A month later, galvanization was started with a constant 100-cell battery. After fifteen months of treating the patient, Prince reported, "The painful condition soon disappeared and has never returned. The ulcer finally healed completely. He has, for a considerable time, performed his customary labor, as a farmer, and enjoys good health."[20]

"With regard to this case, Prince added, "it may be said, that if the growth was not cancerous, but scrofulous, or cachectic, the power of the galvanic current to arrest this last kind of morbid degeneration is at least vindicated. As far as the reproduction of a tumor is evidence of cancer, so far, any agent may be said to be a remedy for cancer, which has the power to arrest this secondary growth."[21]

Prince published thirty-two articles in medical journals between 1866 and 1890, as indexed in the library of the U. S. Army. The articles were published in medical journals of the Illinois State Medical Society, St. Louis Medical Society, American Public Health Association and American Surgical Society, among others. Topics included diphtheria, diseases of the joints, kidney stones, treatment of wounds and club foot.[22]

The Morgan County Medical Society met monthly beginning in 1866. Up to the time Prince died in 1889, he presented 109 reports on topics ranging from public issues of the day to illustrations from his personal practice to material from the Illinois State Medical Society's annual meetings. At the state society's annual meetings, Prince presented thirty-six more reports, including several as chairman of the Surgical Committee. Many of those reports were published in the society's journal and later bound into the books referred to above. Prince presented five papers at annual meetings of the American Medical Association on the topics of ovariotomy, amputation, gangrene, shock and patent rights among medical men.[23]

Professor J. H. Hollister, president of the Illinois State Medical Society, addressed the membership at the twenty-fifth anniversary meeting in Jacksonville in 1875. He reviewed the society's history and recounted the leadership of past presidents and advances in medicine over the period. At one point, he applauded contributions to medical literature that had been written by society members. "With no feigned pleasure do we survey the advancement of the medical profession in our State during this quarter of a century. The medical literature of the State has contributed to this. *The Chicago Medical Journal, The*

Medical Examiner, the writings of Davis, Byford, Prince, Andrews and others, have accomplished an important mission."[24]

ENDNOTES

[1] Prince, David, M.D. *Galvano-Therapeutics. A Revised Reprint of a report made to the Illinois Medical Society.* Philadelphia. Lindsay and Blackiston. 1874. 7.

[2] Black, Carl E., M.D, "David Prince." Unpublished. Read before the Western Surgical Association, Kansas City, MO. 1936. Carl E. Black Papers. Special Collections, Jacksonville, IL Public Library.

[3] Prince. *Orthopedics: A Systematic Treatise upon the Prevention and Correction of Deformities.* Philadelphia. Lindsay & Blakiston. 1866. "Preface."

[4] Prince. *Orthopedics.* 20-24.

[5] Prince. *Plastics: A New Classification and a Brief Exposition of Plastic Surgery.* Philadelphia. Lindsay and Blakiston. 1868. A front insert promoting Prince's 1866 publication of *Orthopedics* listing "Opinions of the press and of the Profession."

[6] Prince. *Orthopedics.* 98.

[7] Prince. *Orthopedics.* 98.

[8] Robinson, Donald. "Sieber, G. A./ Interview and Memoir," taped oral history. Springfield, IL. Archives /Special Collections LIB144. University of Illinois at Springfield. 1954. The interview was with the son of E. R. Sieber.

[9] Prince. *Orthopedics.* 78.

[10] "Dr. Prince's New Work." *Plastics: A New classification and brief exposition of Plastic Surgery.* Front insert. From the *New York Medical Record.* November 15, 1866.

[11] Prince. *Plastics.* 1.

[12] Frank B. Norbury, M. D. "David Prince: The Pioneer in Surgical Therapeutics in Central Illinois." Monograph. The Pearson Museum. Southern Illinois University School of Medicine. Springfield, IL. 1980.

[13] Prince. *Galvano-Therapeutics.* 1, 11.

[14] Prince. *Galvano-Therapeutics.* 7-8.

[15] Prince. *Galvano-Therapeutics.* 16.

[16] Prince. Galvano-Therapeutics. 17.

[17] Prince. Galvano-Therapeutics. 33.

[18] Prince. Galvano-Therapeutics. 25.

[19] Prince. Galvano-Therapeutics. 37.

[20] Prince. Galvano-Therapeutics. 63.

[21] Prince. Galvano-Therapeutics. 42.

[22] Prince. Galvano-therapeutics. 48.

[23] Black, Carl E. "Biographies of Illinois Doctors – D. Prince." Unpublished. Abraham Lincoln Presidential Library.

[24] Holister, J.H., M.D. "A Public Address." Transactions of the Twenty-Fifth Anniversary Meeting of the Illinois State Medical Society. Chicago. 1875.

X
Colleagues in Science

"The professional man has no right to be other than a conscientious student."
Greene Vardiman Black, The
Limitations of Dental Education, 1907

Greene Vardiman Black (1836-1915) was twenty years younger than David Prince, had minimal early education and was known for prodigious self-study as an adult. Ultimately both men received international recognition for pioneering contributions: Prince in orthopedics and plastic surgery, Black in dental practice, nomenclature, preparation of cavities and advances in preparation of amalgam fillings. Black emphasized prevention over repair. According to E. F. Schewe, a G. V. Black biographer, he became "the dominant dental figure of the last half of the nineteenth century and may well still be considered the outstanding personality of the first half of the twentieth."[1]

Figure 13: Greene Vardiman Black. From pioneer to scientist; the life story of Greene Vardiman Black. 1940.

Black grew up on a farm in Cass County, Illinois, near Virginia. He attended school only in winter. At the same time, with the encouragement of his mother, he was an avid reader. His father forbade his entering the nearby Illinois College in Jacksonville. For the Campbellite sectarian, William Black, the college was a "Yankee College of Godless Congregationalism."

At seventeen, Black was sent to study medicine with his brother in Clayton, Adams County. Eleven years older, Dr. Thomas Black graduated from the University of Transylvania Medical College in Louisville, Kentucky. In addition to studying anatomy and medicine with his brother, G. V. Black studied Latin with a local teacher. His social life included playing the trumpet in the local band.[2]

After three years with his brother, Black became a student for four months of Dr. J. C. Speer, a dentist in Mount Sterling, Brown County. The experience led him to prefer practicing dentistry to medicine. He moved to his birthplace, Winchester, to become the first dentist in Scott County. At the time, dentistry was considered a trade, competing with barbers and blacksmiths for pulling teeth. During his five years in Winchester, however, Black developed a thriving practice dealing with extractions, fillings and making lower plates. His records show that in his last year in Winchester he earned $725 in profit from income of $1,213 and expenses of $488. Some payments in lieu of cash included pottery from local craftsmen and produce from farmers.[3]

Of great interest to Black was conducting experiments in metallurgy for fillings. For instance, the problem with gold leaf fillings is that gold is too soft, and gold fillings frequently fall out. Other materials are too hard, leading to cracked teeth. In doing his research, Black visited gunsmiths, blacksmiths, jewelers, and clockmakers. Amalgam fillings – made from a combination of metals that includes mercury, silver, tin, and copper – had been introduced to the United States in 1832, but they were a controversial topic because mercury compounds used by some dentists caused mercury poisoning.[4] The Society of Dental Surgeons in America declared in 1845 that members would be expelled if they used amalgams. Nevertheless, Black continued to work on amalgam fillings without using mercury. It was not until 1895 that he published his final formula, which was adopted by dentists for several decades.[5]

Black also studied the cause and effect of gum and tooth disease in his dental practice. During this independent period, he also studied Latin, French, German and algebra. Black's eldest son, Carl, once wrote in his diary: "I am sometimes bothered with the thought as to whether I will ever acquire the habit of close application to study such as my father has."[6]

After five years in Winchester, Black enlisted for Civil War service in 1862. He was assigned to scouting duties. Dentists were not commissioned in the Union Army; recruits underwent only perfunctory dental examinations to ensure they had opposing front teeth with which to bite off the caps of powder cartridges. (The Confederacy did have commissioned dentists on orders of President Jefferson Davis.) While on scouting duty, Black injured a knee crossing a fence and spent six months in a Kentucky hospital recovering from a subsequent infection. He took advantage of the convalescence to teach himself to write and draw with his left hand.

Shortly after he returned home, Black's wife and one of their two sons died. The surviving son, Carl, went to live with his grandparents in Virginia. Black moved to Jacksonville to establish a partnership with Dr. James C. Cox, who was preparing to retire in November 1864. Black bought out Cox. When he opened the office on his own in January 1865, Black had a ready patient base that increased with patients from Winchester and Virginia he had treated before the Civil War. His first card appearing in the local newspaper was a straightforward announcement of his service and location. Not long after, the following card appeared in the local newspaper:

> *G. V. Black*
> *Dental Surgeon*
> *Laughing Gas – used for extracting teeth*
> *without pain.*
> *Office – north side public square over R. R.*
> *Chambers' Grocery Store.*

Black made his own laughing gas (nitrous oxide) by heating ammonium nitrate. He stored the gas in a double tank set in the corner of his office. However, other dentists criticized Black's newspaper advertisements as unethical – not because he used laughing gas, but because he announced that he did so.[7]

In Jacksonville, Black expanded the dental nomenclature list he had started in Winchester. This list is a classification of caries, instruments, and the characteristics of individual teeth by name, along with abbreviations, precise descriptions, and some drawings. In 1893, when Black was dean of the Northwestern University Dental School, his system for nomenclature and classification was included in a larger list adopted by the faculty. Later that year, Black presented "Report of Committee on Dental Nomenclature" at the World's Columbian Dental Congress in Chicago. The Congress adopted the committee's nomenclature and classifications.

Black continued his self-study of German with the assistance of Edward Weil, a highly educated German clothier with a business near Black's office. Businesses stayed open in the evening, and Black would frequently spend an hour with Weil studying, reading and speaking German. Weil suggested he get a subscription textbook for learning to read German, and Black purchased a German grammar and dictionary. His goal was to be able to read Virchow's *Cellular Pathology* and other books by German authors in the originals. Black's fluency in German and

French led to an invitation from Europeans two decades later to lecture in their forums.[8]

Black's self-education included periodic trips to St. Louis as a member of the St. Louis Dental Society, established in June 1866. The primary attraction was access to the private library of Dr. H. J. McKellops, whose collection at one time was one of the best in the United States. Black was invited to be professor of pathology when the Missouri Dental College opened in St. Louis in 1870. Upon his leaving eight years later, the college granted Black an honorary degree, Doctor of Dental Surgery.[9]

Prince and Black met in Jacksonville after the Civil War. They shared a deep interest in the emerging sciences in Europe, especially germ theory and cell theory. Both had previously adopted the scientific inquiry methods of Charles Darwin. Their interest in the work of their contemporaries is shown by their participation in professional organizations at the state, county, and national levels. Black's ambition was to raise dental practice to a profession. To that end, Black would publish articles only in dental journals and did not attach his name to articles written by Prince about procedures on which they collaborated.

Prince introduced Black to the Morgan County Medical Society at its meeting on December 11, 1866. It was unusual for a dentist to attend, because membership was limited to medical doctors. Black, however, gained some standing when he contributed to Prince's report on anesthetics. The minutes of the meeting summarized the Prince report:

> *Dr. David Prince exhibited several varieties of instruments for producing spray of medication of the air passages and for deadening the sensibilities of parts in order to lessen, or prevent,*

the pain attendant upon surgical or dental operations. He went briefly into the history of the introduction of inhaling medical substances blown off in spray as first practiced in France and Germany and then explained the instrument invented by Dr. Richardson of London for the production of insensibility of parts by blowing upon them a spray of ether or rhingoline, which is capable of freezing in a few seconds by the tendency of rapid evaporation to produce cold. He exhibited an ingenious devise by Dr. G. V. Black for the purpose of shielding the lips and tongue from the spray while it is being blown upon the gums preparatory to extracting teeth.

Dr. Prince referred to cases in which union by the first intention had occurred under unfavorable circumstances after the application of the spray of ether to the cut surfaces. He thought this result was secured by the speedy arrest of the flow of blood from the minute vessels under the influence of cold.

Dr. G. V. Black made some remarks explanatory to his employment of the spray in extracting teeth thinking the instrument a valuable means of lessening or destroying sensibility. In some cases, he had found patients unable to bear the sudden reduction of temperature on account of the exposed and irritable condition of the nerves of the teeth. In some of these cases he had succeeded in employing the spray by first covering the tooth with wax.

"On a motion, it was resolved that the thanks of the society be tendered Dr. Black for his valuable contribution to Dental Surgery.[10]

Black's predilection for sharing his knowledge included publication of a series of articles about diseases of the mouth and teeth in the *Jacksonville Daily Journal* in January 1867. He describes how lodged food particles cause disease and rot of teeth. "Now if these lodgments are prevented, most of the decay will be prevented also. The means of preventing the effects of these lodgments are, happily, in the reach of everyone. The toothbrush will cleanse the most exposed portions, while the toothpick, made of quill or other pliable substance (quill is best), will reach between them and remove all lodgments from them."[11]

Prince and Black also shared interests in microscopes and histology. Microscopes sold for one hundred to eight hundred dollars late in the nineteenth century. Prince purchased one from England. Black traded for a German-made microscope with a German doctor who recently settled in Jacksonville. Black made a case for slides he labeled and numbered. He used material for slides from Prince's surgeries and from patient samples with their consent.

Prince and Greene studied their slides together and decided, in 1876, to initiate a Microscopical Society. The society included seven other doctors, two Illinois College professors, three women and Prince's 22-year-old son Arthur Edward Prince. The society met regularly, usually at a member's home, with each member presenting a different topic. Many meetings were held at Black's home. Black often made drawings of others' sides. Black reportedly collected four thousand slides by the end of his career.[12]

Both men were active in community organizations. Literary society meetings interested them; Prince joined The Club Literary Society and Black joined The Union Literary Society. Both societies met more than once a month. Members represented various professional and businessmen. Black was a member of the Jacksonville Philharmonic Society, playing the violin and the cello. He was also the Third Ward Republican Club chairman for a year in 1878-9. Prince was a member of the School Committee for ten years and donated his annual one hundred dollars stipend to the Jacksonville Library Association to support the free reading room located in donated quarters in the YMCA on West State Street.

Prince and Black had very different personal habits. Prince was a vegetarian, abstained from alcohol and coffee, and never smoked tobacco. Black drank alcohol and consumed large amounts of coffee. In an oral history, his granddaughter, Marjorie Black Drennan, said when he kissed her cheek, she could smell coffee on his beard. Also, Black smoked 150 large black cigars a month. The cigars were manufactured in Jacksonville by Portuguese immigrants.[13]

Black assisted Prince in surgeries, especially those of the face and jaw. In addition, they performed cadaver dissections of the face and jaw, taking tissue samples to examine under a microscope. Prince and Black worked together closely on reconstruction of cleft palates. Cleft palate, a congenital condition, occurs when tissue in the roof of the mouth fails to fuse prior to birth. Reconstruction attempts were few until the last half of the nineteenth century.

In the 1870s, surgeons employed a technique of separating the soft palate tissue and muscles from the hard, bony palate, then sutured the soft palate edges together. In some instances, paste board soaked in castor oil and phenol was used to hold the sutures. By 1875, Prince was closing the suture line with bead sutures on both sides of the cleft tissue. The beads glide on the natural surface and are tightened by twisting a silver wire that passes through the beads. When the soft palate edges meet, they are sutured.[14] "The muscular layers of the soft palate which glide easily upon each other, are kept in their proper positions, and much time is saved," Prince wrote. "The patient is also subjected, for a much shorter time, to the influence of anesthetic inhalations."[15]

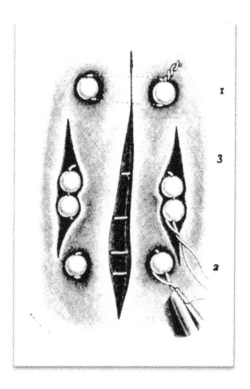

Figure 14: David Prince. "The Bead Suture."
Annals of Anatomy and Surgery.

Nine years later, Black invented pickup needles, which allowed the palate tissue to be joined with thread without endangering deeper tissue and muscles. Prince reported to the Illinois State Medical Society in May of 1884: "By the aid of Dr. G. V. Black, an automatic needle was constructed for the easy and speedy introduction of sutures." Prince also gave the first detailed description of pickup needles in that report. He read his report to the International Medical Congress in Copenhagen in 1884 and also brought sample pickup needles for Europeans to copy.[16]

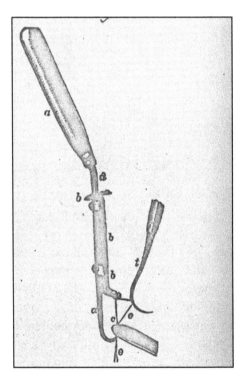

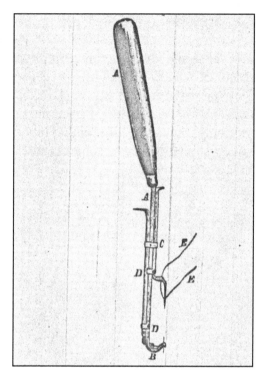

Figure 15. G. V. Black's pick-up needle. G. M. Dorrance, The Operative Story of Cleft Palate.

The success of Prince and Black's procedures was demonstrated by the improvement in speech articulation by patients. "The utility of the closure of the cleft palate, both hard and soft, becomes apparent in every case. Sounds which are impossible with a permanent open communication between the mouth and the pharynx, and especially between the mouth and the nose, become executed with more approximation to perfection," Prince wrote.[17]

The younger the patient, the better, Prince believed. Children one to five years old were ideal candidates for palate reconstruction, "simply because bad habits of articulation are less fixed. When the apparatus of articulation is restored, the patient must learn anew how to use it. Unless the greatest care and caution are observed, combined with instruction in minute detail, the restored organs will never attain a performance equal to their capabilities." To illustrate a successful cleft palate closure, Prince presented the state medical society with a ten-year-old boy who had surgery when he was seven. After the boy read for the audience of physicians, Prince commented: "You notice that his utterance of all the vocal sounds is perfect, and he can whistle, which implies that the palate comes against the posterior wall of the pharynx and completely closes the communication with the posterior nostrils."[18]

Prince's pioneering efforts in reconstruction of the cleft palate were included in *The Operative Story of Cleft Palate* (1933) by George Morris Dorrance, a Philadelphia surgeon. In answering a 1935 letter from Prince biographer Carl Black, Dorrance wrote: "Dr. Prince was the first one in the Mississippi valley to be interested in these subjects."[19]

While remaining based in Jacksonville, G.V. Black traveled to lecture at dental schools in Iowa and Chicago in the late 1880s. In 1891, he moved from Jacksonville to Chicago to teach at Northwestern University Dental School. Rising to the position of dean of the dental school, he remained at Northwestern until his death in 1915. Among Black's longest-lasting contributions to dental practice is the principle of "Extension for Prevention," coined by Black in an 1893 report on cavities. It describes removing all decay from a tooth by extending preparation beyond the decay, leaving a solid and smooth surface for attachment of a filling. This basic principle has survived to modern times.[20] G. V. Black is still considered "the father of modern dentistry."

ENDNOTES

[1] Schewe. E. F. *Greene Vardiman Black – The Man of the Centuries*. Bernard Becker Medical Library. St. Louis. Washington University School of Dental Medicine. 2002.
[2] Black, Carl E. and Bessie M. *From Pioneer to Scientist – The Life Story of Greene Vardiman Black*. 24.
[3] Black, Bessie M. "Greene Vardiman Black 1836-1915." Transactions of the Illinois State Historical Society for the year 1932. 80.
[4] Black, Carl E. and Bessie M. *From Pioneer to Scientist – The Life Story of Greene Vardiman Black*.122.
[5] Donelan, James C., DDS. "Greene Vardiman Black – Here He Grew in Greatness." G. V. Black District Dental Society. Jacksonville, IL 1960. Jacksonville Public Library; Thorpe, Burton Lee, M. D., D. D. S. "Greene Vardiman Black, M. D., D. D. S., Sc. D., LL. D. The Leading Contributor to Modern Scientific Dentistry." *History of Dental Surgery*. Vol 2. Chicago. National Art Publishing Co. 1909. 559-589 passim; "Dentistry." *Encyclopedia of Children and Childhood in History and Society*. 2004. The Gale Group Inc. https://www.encyclopedia.com/medicine/divisions-diagnostics-and-procedures/medicine/dentistry.
[6] Black, Carl E. "Diary." C. E. Black Papers. Abraham Lincoln Presidential Library. Box 14 April 25,1885.
[7] Black, Carl E. and Bessie M. *From Pioneer to Scientist – The Life Story of Greene Vardiman Black*.122.
[8] Black, Carl E. and Bessie M. *From Pioneer to Scientist – The Life Story of Greene Vardiman Black*.145.
[9] Black, Carl E. and Bessie M. *From Pioneer to Scientist – The Life Story of Greene Vardiman Black*.161.

[10] "History of Medicine" *Jacksonville Daily Journal*. April 11, 1917. Jacksonville, IL. 4. Edited by Dr. Walter Frank, Secretary of the Morgan County Medical Society.

[11] Black, Carl E. and Bessie M. *From Pioneer to Scientist – The Life Story of Greene Vardiman Black.* 124-125.

[12] Eames, Charles M. *Historic Morgan and Classic Jacksonville.* 1884-'85. The *Daily Journal* steam job printing office, Jacksonville, IL. 1885. 22. The original of this book is in the Cornell University Library.

[13] Drennan, Marjorie Black. "Memoir." Interview by Barbara Gross, 1974. Archives/Special Collections LIB 144. University of Illinois Springfield. Springfield, IL.

[14] Black, Carl E. and Bessie M. *From Pioneer to Scientist – The Life Story of Greene Vardiman Black.* 207-208.

[15] Prince, David. "The Bead Suture – A modification of the quilled Suture for Palatoplasty, and for use in other situations with which the suture line requires to be supported for several days." Brooklyn, N.Y. *Annals of Anatomy and Surgery*. Volume VII. January -June. 1883. 143.

[16] Prince. "The Bead Suture." 146.

[17] Prince. "The Bead Suture." 143.

[18] Prince. "Palatoplastry." Transactions of the Thirty-Fourth Annual Meeting of the Illinois State Medical Society. Chicago. 1884. 141.

[19] G. M. Dorrance to Carl E. Black. December 30, 1935. Carl E. Black Papers. Box 14. Abraham Lincoln Presidential Library. Springfield, IL.

[20] Black, Carl E. and Bessie M. *From Pioneer to Scientist – The Life Story of Greene Vardiman Black.* 244.

XI
Prince Remembered

"On review, the brilliance of this surgeon stands out most emphatically amongst his colleagues. He dealt in both general and orthopedic surgery and had time to do much experimental work under very crude conditions."

Kellogg Speed, *History of Medical Practice in Illinois, 1850-1900*

David Prince reached the pinnacle of his career in the 1880s, attending two European sessions of the International Medical Congress. In the 1884 Congress, he presented new methods and instruments for reconstruction of a cleft palate. Upon returning, he extended his sanitarium building by attaching an air-purified surgery room. The impetus to construct a surgical theater was inspired by his visits to hospitals in London, Paris, Berlin and Copenhagen. In addition, he visited the laboratories of Lister and Pasteur.

A highlight of his 1881 trip was the opportunity he took to see the Museum of the Royal College of Surgeons in London. The main attraction for Prince was an area devoted to John Hunter (1728-1793). Hunter was a Scottish surgeon and early advocate of the scientific method in medicine. Since his early medical studies, Prince had been aware of Hunter's writing and reputation as a pioneer in anatomy and dissection. The museum displayed an extensive collection of Hunter's anatomical specimens. In his diary of the trip, Prince paid special attention to the museum area dedicated to Hunter:

> *London, Sunday Aug. 7. Museum of the Royal College of Surgeons.*
>
> *The nucleus of the Museum is (according to Baedeker) 10,000 preparations made by John Hunter. At the room first entered is a statue, in marble, of John Hunter, by Weeks, and whether or not it has any resemblance to Hunter it is a fine representation of a face and attitude in the act of thinking. We can easily imagine that this was his attitude while working out some of his physiological and pathological problems. Some collections of teeth are very interesting, made by Hunter himself. One of the recent acquisitions of the museum is the clothing and watch of a man struck by lightning while standing under a tree. He was stripped naked without being hurt, the clothing and shoes being very much torn and the watch broken. The shoes of a laboring man had heavy nails in their soles and he was not wet by rain.*
>
> *The museum is rich in specimens of diseased and injured bones including deformities from rickets, long bones bent and spine curved. Some fine examples of neurosis and a remarkable example of spina Ventosa in the anterior end of the lower jaw of jaw of a pig probably resulting from the distention by pus resulting from diseased tooth, though the front teeth and the alveolar ridge do not appear in the specimen. The other side of the jaw is not shown.[1]*

In addition to traveling, operating his sanitarium, writing and attending professional meetings, Prince was involved with the Passavant Hospital in Jacksonville from the time it opened in 1875. The hospital started as an adjunct to an orphans' home that opened in 1868, when Jacksonville resident Eliza Ayers collaborated with Rev. William A. Passavant on the project. Mrs. Ayers purchased the former Berean College property on East State Street at a sheriff's sale. Passavant, a Lutheran minister from Pittsburgh, operated eight hospitals in the United States, including one in Chicago. When the property was vested in The Association for Works of Mercy of the Evangelical Lutheran Church of Illinois the orphan home project moved ahead. A biographer quotes Passavant as saying: "The awful discomforts, poverty and makeshifts of those years of struggle are known only to God and to a few faithful souls. Through it all and to his death, Dr. Prince was a friend of the Institution."[2]

Prince reduced his activity in 1889, though still spending most of his time at the sanitarium every day. He also remained active in the county medical society, where he gave his last report in July on "Fibroid Tumor." When the Illinois State Medical Society held its annual meeting in Jacksonville in May, Prince gave a report on "Hedge Thorn Poison."[3]

The Osage Orange (*Maclura pomifera*) hedge involved in the Prince report is not native to Central Illinois. It was introduced as a windbreak and fencing for farm buildings and confinements. The fruit of the hedge is a yellowish-green ball, about the size of an orange, with thorns; when it pricks the skin, it can cause severe infection. Jonathan Baldwin Turner, a teacher at Illinois College and a close friend of Prince, introduced the Osage Orange hedge to central Illinois – he started with seeds he was given by a circuit-riding preacher who had seen the plant on the banks of the Osage River in Arkansas. Turner grew and sold Osage Orange hedge as one of his agriculture projects. (Turner eventually left Illinois College, but he pursued his interest in agriculture and agricultural education. He became a leader in the land-grant college movement.)[4]

Prince viewed hedge thorn poisoning as a study in antiseptic surgery. He described the hedge thorn as becoming poisonous when septic germs floating in the air adhere to the tiny thorn, which breaks off as it enters living tissue. A 52-year-old man came to Prince two weeks after a hedge thorn pricked his right hand, which had become red and swollen. Prince first treated it with a poultice. In a few days, a knot formed on the right forearm, which also became swollen and painful. Iodine and carbolic acid were injected into the knot. At this point, Prince resorted to "radical" antiseptic surgery to deal with internal sepsis. "Free and numerous incisions, subcutaneous injections of iodoform in ether, subcutaneous injections of carbolic acid, washing out sinuses and abscesses with solutions of sublimate, cinnamon, boric acid and peroxide of hydrogen; injecting with antiseptic solutions, or enveloping in dry boric acid when the internal sepsis has been subdued, are among the local measures," Prince wrote. He summed up the treatment by adding that septic microbes weakened by antiseptic agents allow leucocytics (white blood cells) to destroy the foreign element. "People who suffer evil consequences from this apparently slight accident, are impressed with the idea of a poison connected with the thorn," Prince wrote.[5]

Prince was busy seeing patients and working in his office up to five days before he died. The Saturday before his death was a rainy, chilly December day, but Prince walked the seven blocks to and from his home and the sanitarium. He felt a chill when he arrived home at 9 p.m. He ate dinner and went to bed. Sunday morning, he attempted to dress himself and go to the office, but found he could not and went back to bed. On Monday, Dr. T. J. Pitner and other physicians diagnosed Prince's condition as pneumonia. His condition deteriorated, and he died at 7:20 p.m. Thursday, December 19, 1889. One obituary reported: "His son, Dr. A. E. Prince, informs he had never been confined to his bed but once, and that for few days, about thirty years ago, with an attack of pneumonia."[6]

The next day, both Jacksonville newspapers, the *Daily Journal* and the *Daily Courier*, devoted lengthy columns to his obituary. The Journal published an editorial expressing the management's grief at Prince's death. The editorial noted he had been one of the directors of the company and said he "was of the very greatest service to the enterprise; his advice was frequently sought and freely given." The editorial praised Prince's generosity and said he never heralded his contributions: "hundreds have had occasion to bless the doctor, not only for his aid physically but financially as well."[7]

In Springfield, The *Illinois State Journal* praised Prince as being "known all over the state as a surgeon of high standing and a benevolent gentleman and had the respect and regard of every doctor in the State and all the citizens." Of the sanitarium, the Journal said, "This institution might have been a source of great wealth but owing to Dr. Prince's benevolent spirit it probably harbored as many charity patients as paying patients during its history." The obituary noted that a large group of physicians and friends would travel from Springfield on a special train to attend Prince's funeral.[8] News of the death of David Prince received wide circulation in the necrologies of many national medical journals. In addition to the *Journal of Illinois State Medical Society*, some others were *The Cincinnati Lancet Clinic, The Carolina Medical Journal* and *The Journal of the American Medical Association.* The plaudits outlined his contributions to plastic surgery and orthopedics, in addition to his prolific publication of books and articles. Also, Prince was commended for his volunteer service with the Army of the Potomac.

All the journals pointed to Prince's contributions to advances in surgery. A 1994 article in the *Journal of American Society of Plastic Surgeons* emphasized his groundbreaking 1868 book on plastic surgery: "His contributions were important to the dissemination of plastic surgery," the article said. It also noted Prince's reports to the U. S. Sanitary Commission after the Civil War, in which he concluded there were few plastic surgery applications. "His reasoning may have been based partly on the fact that plastic surgery, as he knew it, entailed difficult, protracted procedures, not what could easily be adapted to acute wounds or battlefield conditions, where immediate treatment was inadequate and triage was considerably delayed."[9]

The day after Prince died, nearly 100 people attended a tribute at Conservatory Hall organized by a variety of prominent citizens of Jacksonville. Those attending adopted four resolutions of praise and recognition. One resolution called for the mayor and city council to name the library and reading room at the YMCA the David Prince Free Public Library. It was offered to recognize Prince's generosity in donating his school board stipend to the library. However, the city council already had amended the city tax levy to include support of the free library and reading room and had renamed it the Jacksonville Public Library, so no action was taken on the request to recognize Prince.[10]

At a special meeting, the Jacksonville School Board adopted a resolution honoring Prince. It was not until 1913 that Prince received enduring recognition: a newly constructed building was named the David Prince Junior High School. Classes were held there until 1957, after which it was used for administrative purposes until the building was demolished in 1983.[11]

Jacksonville Mayor James T. King asked all members of the city council and board of education to attend Prince's funeral in a body. Prince's colleagues from The Club Literary Society likewise agreed to attend the funeral as a group.

The Funeral

The crowd at Prince's funeral, held at 2 p.m. Sunday, December 22, packed the Congregational Church and then some. Many attendees waited outside. "The entire number in attendance must have been between two and three thousand and the assemblage represented all ranks and conditions, all vocations and trades, all sects, all colors, all ages, and both sexes," the *Daily Courier* reported. After the family and friends were seated, the casket, covered with rare flowers, was borne by eight prominent men, including Prince's colleague, Dr. G. V. Black.[12]

The service was led by Rev. F. S. Hayden and Edward A. Tanner, president of Illinois College. Hayden's remarks centered on Prince's "gifts of healing," his many admirable traits and "power to attract strong affections." Tanner's eulogy included more personal comments:

> *One night, a dozen years ago, we sat up till into the small hours of the morning, discussing revealed religion and especially, the revelation of God in Christ. His words and bearing were earnest and reverent. Our creeds were in part concurrent, in part divergent, and we bade each other good-bye, saying that, whichever was right and whichever was wrong, if we could preserve that same spirit of patient docility, we should at*

length be guided to a knowledge of all essential truth. ...

Though skeptical in his tendencies, (Prince) became so impressed with the evidences of adaption and design that were forced upon him, by his constant examination of the frame work of the body, that he was brought at last to subscribe, most reverently, to the doctrine of an omnipotent and omniscient Creator.

Commenting on Prince's relations with Illinois College, Tanner quoted Prince as saying: "'Come to me whenever there is a project on foot to render the college a greater blessing.' More than once has he sought an opportunity to make a generous donation before he was approached on the subject," Tanner said.[13]

At the close of the service, the people outside came in to view Prince's casket. Those seated waited a half hour for the mourners to pass through. A long line of mourners followed the casket two miles to the Diamond Grove Cemetery. Tanner and Hayden led a second, brief ceremony at the cemetery.[14]

David Prince, during his time in Jacksonville, collected more than two hundred rare photographs of historically prominent persons in Jacksonville and Morgan County. The photographs are pasted on cardboard pages of an album. Included in the album are: Julian Sturtevant and wife; Rev. Sherwood Eddy, former pastor of the First Presbyterian Church; Drs. Hiram K. Jones and Samuel Adams, early local physicians and Prince colleagues at the Illinois College Medical Department; Joel Morton and wife, who settled in Jacksonville in 1817; and John Carson, the first child born in Jacksonville. The album passed to David Prince's son, Dr. Arthur Prince, who donated the album to the

Jacksonville Public Library in 1904 and is currently held in the library's Special Collections.[15]

ENDNOTES

[1] Papers of Carl E. Black. Box 15. "Biographies of Illinois Doctors – David Prince." Copy of David Prince Diary – Trip to Europe 1881. Abraham Lincoln Presidential Library. Springfield, Illinois.

[2] Gerberding, G. H., D. D. *Life and Letters of W. A. Passavant,* D. D. Greenville, PA. The Young Lutheran Co. 1906. 488.

[3] Papers of Carl E. Black. Box 14. "Bibliography". Abraham Lincoln Presidential Library. Springfield, Illinois.

[4] Carriel, Mary Turner. *The Life of Jonathan Baldwin Turner.* Copyright Mary T. Carriel. 1911. 65-69.

[5] Prince, David. "The Hedge Thorn Poison." *Transactions of the Thirty-Ninth Annual Meeting of the Illinois State Medical Society.* May 1889. 169-172.

[6] "Dr. Prince Dead." *Jacksonville Daily Courier.* December 25, 1889.

[7] Editorial." *Jacksonville Daily Journal.* December 20, 1889.

[8] "Dr. David Prince." *The Illinois State Journal.* December 21, 1889.

[9] Goldwyn, Robert M., M. D. and Ossoff, Robert H. "David Prince, 1816-1889." *Plastic and Reconstructive Surgery: Journal of American Society of Plastic Surgeons.* June 1994. 1514 - 1518.

[10] "Dr. Prince Eulogized" *Jacksonville Daily Journal.* December 22, 1889; "History of the Jacksonville Public Library." Jacksonville Public Library. jaxpl.org/history.asp.

[11] Mann, Jewell and Crowe, Robert. *Rich History Bright Future 150 Years of Jacksonville School District #117.* Jacksonville School District. 2018. 44-45.

[12] "The City Mourns." *Jacksonville Daily Journal.* Monday, December 23, 1889.

[13] Tanner, Edward Allen, D.D. "A Great Physician." *Baccalaureate and Other Sermons, and Addresses.* Chicago and New York. Fleming H. Revell Company. 1892.

[14] "The City Mourns." *Jacksonville Daily Courier.* December 23, 1889.

[15] "A Choice Gift." *Jacksonville Daily Journal.* January 29, 1904.

XII
David Prince Legacy

*"It has the usual quota of excellent hospitals –
the Springfield Hospital and St. John's Hospital,
standing high among the institutions of the state.
Here too, the Illinois State Board of Health
maintains its hygienic laboratories and carries out
it notable sanitary and public health work. More
interesting and more out of the ordinary, however,
stands the David Prince Sanitarium, which has the
distinction of being the largest private hospital for
the treatment of the eye, ear, nose and throat to be
found in the United States or, in all probability, in
the world."*

Chicago Clinic Pure Water
Journal, January 1908

Both sons of David Prince joined their father's practice after
gaining medical degrees followed by study in Europe. Dr. Arthur
Prince returned to Illinois in 1877, specializing in eye, ear, nose
and throat ailments. Dr. John Prince entered the practice in 1887
as a surgeon. Despite David Prince's reputation in
ophthalmology, Arthur assumed his father's ophthalmological
patients. The arrangement permitted his father to devote more
time to general surgery, which at the time he found more
interesting.[1]

Prince's sons developed an interest in practicing in Springfield before their father's death. Arthur married a Springfield woman, Charlotte Hitchcock, in 1887 and visited Springfield twice a week to see patients. On Jan. 4, 1890, within two weeks of their father's funeral, the Illinois State Journal published a brief article announcing that Drs. Arthur and John Prince were seeking property for the purpose of moving the David Prince Sanitarium from Jacksonville to Springfield.

John left for Europe early in 1890 to further his surgical studies in preparation for his role in the new sanitarium. Arthur stayed home to manage the Jacksonville sanitarium and continue the search for desirable property in Springfield. When John returned from Europe in September, the brothers bought a four-story residence on the southwest corner of Seventh Street and Capitol Avenue in Springfield for nine thousand dollars. On October 11, David Prince's widow, Lucy, sold the Jacksonville sanitarium property on South Sandy Street for six thousand dollars to Dr. Thomas Johnson Whitten of Nokomis. Whitten was widely known in Central Illinois as a physician and surgeon.[2]

By the end of 1890, the brothers had established the David Prince Sanitarium in the remodeled building at Seventh and Capitol. Springfield's population in 1890 was 24,963. The city was experiencing a construction boom, and the David Prince Sanitarium was considered an important addition. In the ensuing decade, the brothers expanded the facility, culminating in a four-story brick building with a frontage of 157 feet facing Capitol Avenue.[3]

The sanitarium's first floor, a half basement, held offices rented to a physiotherapist and podiatrist, along with the facility's kitchen and dining room. Patients had the option, if able, to eat in the dining room as long as he or she was accompanied by a relative. Patients unable to leave their rooms had their meals served by nurses.

The main reception area on the second floor was made up of rooms to interview and examine new patients. Sanitarium staff offices also were on the second floor, as well as post-operative recovery rooms and a room for pathological work.

Three surgery theaters occupied the middle of the third floor, with the remaining rooms for patients. In addition to describing the sanitarium space organization, visitors from the *Chicago Clinic Pure Water Journal* described the three adjoining operating rooms as "most excellent with north light and with electric lighting in frosted lamps so perfect that the night light is even better than that by day. The walls, floors and ceilings are in white tile and the bases and cases in white marble." [4]

The fourth floor had more rooms for patients and a dormitory for out-of-town family and friends. The dormitory provided various room sizes, all with lavatories.

Figure 16: David Prince Sanitarium. Springfield, Illinois. Clinical Notes of The David Prince Sanitarium. *Dr. Arthur Prince. 1907.*

Figure 17: Private room with bath. Clinical Notes.

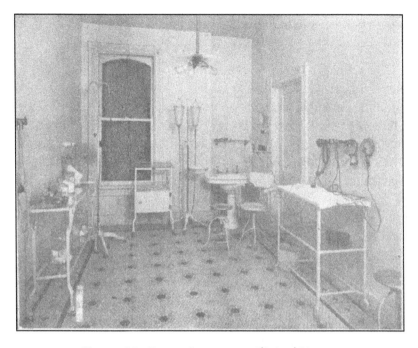

Figure 18: Operating room. Clinical Notes.

John Prince performed surgeries in the largest of the three theaters. He was also a consultant to many hospitals in the state. When the Springfield Hospital (today's Memorial Medical Center) opened in 1899, John Prince contracted to be a staff surgeon there and moved his patients to the new hospital. He kept only a consultation office at the Prince Sanitarium. Thereafter, the sanitarium became known for serving patients seeking treatments for eye, ear, nose and throat problems. That apparently didn't affect demand for sanitarium services. Arthur Prince wrote in the 1907 publication *Clinical Notes*: "During the following years it has been found necessary to increase the capacity, which has been done by rearrangements and an addition, until it now has accommodations for seventy-five house patients. It is provided with inter-communicating telephones, electric annunciator system, Stalimon lavatories, X-Ray laboratory, baths and all that goes to make up a modern institution."[5]

The Springfield City Directory for 1907 listed a staff of eleven under the direction of Arthur Prince. One of those was Dr. Ninus S. Penick, a graduate of Northwestern University and Rush Medical College who had done postgraduate study in London and Berlin. He brought a special interest in eye, ear, nose and throat illnesses, but was not involved in surgeries. He spent much of his time in medical ophthalmology and refractions. Penick remained at the Prince Sanitarium until his death in 1928. The rest of the 1907 staff included three nurses, a bookkeeper, a stenographer, a matron, two waitresses, a maid and a cook.[6]

Operating days were Monday, Thursday, and Saturday. A clinic was open once a month at which physicians from Springfield and elsewhere in central Illinois typically saw twenty to thirty patients. On the December 6, 1907 clinic day at the sanitarium, local physicians were joined by physicians from Peoria, Mount Pulaski, Atlanta, El Paso, Edinburg, Ashland, Virginia and Lincoln. Arthur Prince performed some of the operations, which included cataract extractions, tonsillectomies, sinus drainage and correcting nose deformities. Arthur, in the mold of his father, often utilized instruments of his own design and did not charge poor patients.[7]

In addition to their medical practices, the Prince brothers invested in real estate in Illinois and other states. In 1903, Arthur Prince bought 3,000 acres in Arkansas with two others. He sold several properties in Jacksonville previously. John Prince and three others from Springfield sold 5,000 acres of timber in Nebraska in 1907. The land, purchased for five dollars per acre, was sold for twenty dollars per acre.[8]

The brothers also were socially and professionally prominent. They were members of the Sangamon County Medical Society, the Illinois State Medical Society and the American Medical Association. In addition, Arthur Prince had a legislative appointment as a trustee of the Illinois Charitable Eye and Ear Infirmary in Chicago. He boosted the 1910 Illinois State Fair by sponsoring a banquet for traveling salesmen in April at the St. Nicholas Hotel. Friday, October 7, 1910 was Traveling Men's Day at the state fair.[9]

Dr. John Prince, age 47, died suddenly of a heart attack at home on January 1, 1911. He was survived by his wife, daughter and son. The Prince family received condolences from professional organizations and individuals. "Few men of Central Illinois were so widely known or as generally popular as Doctor John Prince. In his profession, he ranked as one of the leading surgeons of the state and his services and advice were sought in many extraordinary cases," the *Jacksonville Daily Journal* said. Prince was buried at Oak Ridge Cemetery in Springfield.[10]

Arthur Prince continued to operate the sanitarium. In the following decade, however, the patient population began to decline, falling to about thirty by the early 1920s. Prince rented more space to area physicians as well as to a public restaurant on the first floor, replacing the institutional kitchen and dining room.

Catastrophe struck the afternoon of August 23, 1923, when fire engulfed the third and fourth floors of the sanitarium. Five nurses helped twenty-five patients to escape. Seriously ill patients were immediately taken to the First Presbyterian Church across the street and later moved to St. John's Hospital.

Damage was estimated to be between forty and fifty thousand dollars. The two upper floors suffered from the fire itself, while the bottom two floors experienced only smoke and water damage. Some records, valuable instruments and books were removed from the building during the fire.[11]

The building was insured, and Prince announced two days later that it would be rebuilt "in a thoroughly modern, fireproof manner." The sanitarium reopened after restoration, and Arthur Prince continued his practice.

A contributor to *History of Medical Practice in Illinois* who spent a day with Prince in 1926 described him as having an unusual personality. The contributor witnessed Prince perform seven surgical procedures by the end of the day. "He was an enthusiastic and tireless worker who delighted in a waiting room full of patients and a full day in the operating room," the observer wrote. "Such a man was bound to have enemies, especially since he made a practice of frequently visiting other cities in the state, where he would see many patients and perform operations, much to the consternation and jealousy of the local specialists."[12]

In 1927, Prince transferred sole ownership of the sanitarium building to his wife Charlotte, and the First National Bank of Springfield took over management of the property. Prince, however, continued to work at the sanitarium until the summer of 1930 when he became ill. At that point, Prince retired and closed the David Prince Sanitarium.

Dr. Arthur Prince, 76, died October 21, 1930 at his home in Springfield. He was survived by his wife, a son and two daughters. Funeral services were held at his home, followed by interment at Diamond Grove Cemetery in Jacksonville. In the necrology of the *Journal of the Illinois State Historical Society*, it was said of Arthur Prince: "Probably there is not a town between Joliet and Cairo in which the 'Prince' name does not mean in the minds of a large number of people the final authority upon eye troubles. He had a great capacity for work. Dr. Prince appeared to be able to see and dispose of more patients in a day than two other men."[13]

The former sanitarium was converted to a rental building that primarily housed offices of various medical providers and residential apartments. Charlotte Prince sold the property in September 1947 for $127,000 to a trust managed by the First National Bank of Springfield.

As the building aged and declined, its tenants were more likely to be low-income, and finally, in 1977, Springfield building inspectors determined the building no longer met safety standards. By then, the remaining tenants were a physician, an optical services company and a real estate agent, along with about a dozen mostly elderly residents. The former David Prince Sanitarium was demolished in 1978.[14]

ENDNOTES

[1] Davis, David J., Editor. "Early Illinois Ophthalmologists Outside the Chicago Area." *History of Medical Practice in Illinois Vol. II: 1850-1900*. Chicago. The Illinois State Medical Society. The Lakeside Press, R. R. Donnelley & Sons. 1955. 276.

[2] *The Illinois State Journal*. September 13, 1890. 4; Morgan County Clerk's Records Office. Grantors. Book 46. Page 147; Taylor, Jacob L. "T. J. Whitten." *Past and Present of Montgomery County, Illinois*. Chicago. S. J. Clarke Publishing Company. 1904, Updated October 27, 2012.

[3] Patton, Robert Jess, M. D. "Robert Jess Patton Memoir." Archives/Special Collections LIN 144. University of Illinois at Springfield. Springfield, Illinois. Interviewed by Eugenia Eberle, 1993-1993. University of Illinois Board of Trustees. 1993. Robert Patton's father treated Dr. John Prince's patients after his death.

[4] "A Clinic at the David Prince Sanitarium." *The Chicago Clinic Pure Water Journal*. January 1908.

[5] Prince, Arthur. *Clinical Notes of the David Prince Sanitarium*. Self-published. 1907. 3.

[6] Davis. *History of Medical Practice in Illinois*. 276; *Springfield City Directory*. 1907. Southfield, Michigan. R.L. Polk & Company.

[7] "A Clinic at the David Prince Sanitarium." *The Chicago Clinic Pure Water Journal*. January 1908. Passim.

[8] "Springfield Men in Big Timber Deal." *Decatur Herald*. July 30, 1907.

[9] "State News in Brief." *The Daily Herald*. Chicago. August 15, 1903; "New Atoms." *The Times*. Streator, Illinois. April 21, 1910.

[10] "Dr. John Prince Dead." *Jacksonville Daily Journal*. January 3, 1911.

[11] "Sanitarium Is Hit by Blaze; Patients Flee." *Daily Illinois State Journal.* August 24, 1923; "Plan Rebuilding of Sanitarium." *Daily Illinois State Journal.* August 25, 1923.
[12] Davis, David J., editor. "Early Illinois Ophthalmologists Outside the Chicago Area." *History of Medical Practice in Illinois Vol. II: 1850-1900.* Chicago. The Illinois State Medical Society. The Lakeside Press, R. R. Donnelley & Sons. 1955. 276.
[13] "Dr. Prince is Taken by Death in Springfield." *The Daily Journal.* Jacksonville, Illinois. October 22, 1930; "Dr. Arthur E. Prince. 1854-1930." *Journal of the Illinois State Historical Society* Vol. 24, No. 1. April 1931. 163-164.
[14] Sangamon County Clerk records; *State Journal-Register.* December 7, 1977.

Afterword

Although medical specialties were not common in the nineteenth century, David Prince was recognized as a leading surgeon in plastic surgery, ophthalmology and orthopedics. His medical education with surgeons in the East led to Prince, at twenty-four, being reported as the first in Illinois to successfully remove an ovarian tumor. By the end of his career, Prince had achieved international recognition for his innovations in cleft palate repair.

In Jacksonville, Illinois, Prince was more than a country doctor. His medical/surgical practice included proctoring students preparing for medical school. At the Illinois College Medical Department, he loaned funds to students, and in private practice he often took on students for free, sometimes in small groups. His generosity extended to treating indigent patients without charge. Prince also found time to contribute to the community by serving on the school board and participating in public discussions of current events.

It was after Prince enlisted as a volunteer in the Union Army during the Civil War that he became a prodigious writer and expanded his practice with the opening of a sanitarium. He was a leader in medical societies, not only working with others to improve the practice of medicine, but also to fight for professional standing through state legislative enactments.

More than a century after Prince's death, he is still mentioned in medical journals. A 1994 article in the *Journal of American Society of Plastic Surgeons* wrote: "A once significant but now generally forgotten figure in the development of plastic surgery in America during the nineteenth century is David Prince."

The medical career of David Prince embodied the comment of his collaborator, the dental innovator G. V. Black: "The professional man has no right to be other than a conscientious student."

Appendix A

Medical books returned to Illinois College by the American College of Surgeons

This is a list of historic and rare books donated to Illinois College Schewe Library, Jacksonville, IL in 2013 by the American College of Surgeons, Chicago. These books were donated to the ACS in 1941 by the Morgan County (IL) Medical Society. All the books have faceplates for the Morgan County Medical Society Library including five with additional faceplates for the Illinois College Medical Department (1843-1848). The list begins with the five titles originally belonging to Illinois College and eleven originally from the private library of Dr. David Prince that was donated to the Morgan County Medical Society by his son, Dr. Arthur E. Prince.

Titles with Illinois College Medical Department faceplates:

1. Ferriar, John, M.D. *Medical Histories and Reflections.* Philadelphia. Thomas Dobson. 1816.
2. Gregory, John. L., M.D., F.R.S., First Physician to his Royal Majesty of Scotland. *Lectures on the Duties and Qualifications of a Physician.* Philadelphia. M. Carey & Son. 1817.
3. Hillary, William, M.D. *Observations on the Changes of the Air, and the Concomitant Epidemical Diseases in the Island of Barbadoes / A Treatise on the Putrid Bilious Fever, Commonly Called the Yellow Fever.* Philadelphia. B. & T. Kite. 1811.

4. Hoffmann, Johann Moritz. *Idea Machinae Humae Anatomico-physiologia*. Altdorf, Germany. 1703. Latin text with illustrations.
5. Parsons, Usher, M.D. Professor of Anatomy and Surgery, Brown University. *Boylston Prize Dissertations*. Boston, MA. Charles C. Little and James Brown Publishers. 1839. Dissertations on: 1. Inflamation of the periosteum; 2. Eneuresis irrita; 3. Cutaneous diseases; 4. Cancer of the breast. Also, remarks on animal and vegetable decompositions.

Titles containing the signature of David Prince from his personal library:

6. Ashhurst, John Jr. *Injuries of the Spine*. Philadelphia. J. B. Lippincott & Company. 1864.
7. Beard, George M. *Stimulants and Narcotics*. New York. G. P. Putnam & Sons. 1871.
8. Bigalow, Henry Jacob, M.D. *Manual of Orthopedic Surgery*. Boston. William D. Tickner & Company. 1845. Boylston Prize 1844.
9. Butler, John, M.D. *Electricity in Surgery*. New York. Boericke & Tafel. 1882.
10. Cadell, T., editor. *Medical Observations*, Vol. 4. Society of Physicians. London. 1784.
11. Hale, E. Jr. *History and description of an epidemic fever, commonly called Spotted Fever, which prevailed at Gardiner, Maine, in the Spring of 1814*. Boston. Wells and Lilly. 1818.
12. Larrey, D. J. *Observations on wounds, and their complications by erysipelas, gangrene and tetanus, and on the principal diseases and injuries of the head, ear and eye*. Philadelphia. Mielke & Biddle. 1832.

13. Ramsay, David. *An Eulogium upon Benjamin Rush / Professor of the institutes and practice of medicine and of clinical practice in the University of Pennsylvania; who departed this life April 19, 1813, in the sixty-ninth year of his age.* Philadelphia. Bradford and Inskeep. 1813. Bought at auction by David Prince in St. Louis in 1851.

14. Serre, Par M. *Traité Sur L'Art De Restaurer Les Difformités De La Face Selon La Methode Par Déplacement ou Methode Française.* Paris. Lours Castel. 1842.

15. Society of Physicians in London. *Medical Observations an Inquires by a Society of Physicians in London.* Vol. 5. London. T. Cadell. 1784.

16. Van Buren, W. H., A.M.M.D. *Diseases of the Rectum.* New York. D. Appleton and Company 1870.

Titles containing faceplates of the Morgan County Medical Society:

17. Allen, John. *Synopsis Medicinae: or, a Summary View of the Whole Practice of Physick.* London. C. Hitch and L. Hawes. 1761.

18. Baillie. Matthew. *The Morbid Anatomy of Some of the Most Important Parts of the Human Body.* Albany. Thomas Spencer. 1745.

19. Barnwell, William. *Physical Investigations & Deductions, from Medical and Surgical Facts.* Philadelphia. W. W. Woodward. 1802.

20. Beaumont, William. *Experiments and Observations on the Gastric Juice, and the Physiology of Digestion.* Boston. Lilly, Wait and Company. 1834.

21. Bedford, Gunning S. Clinical Lectures on the Diseases of Women and Children. New York. William Wood & Company. 1866.
22. Bell, Benjamin, M.D. *A System of Surgery*. Philadelphia. Thomas Dobson. 1806. Extracted from the works of Benjamin Bell, of Edinburgh: by Nicholas Waters, M.D., Fellow of the College of Physicians of Philadelphia, and one of he surgeons of the Philadelphia Dispensary.
23. Bell, Charles. *A Series of Engravings, Explaining the Course of the Nerves*. Philadelphia. Anthony Finley. 1818. With an address to young physicians on the study of the nerves.
24. Bennett, John Hughes. *The Pathology Treatment of Pulmonary Tuberculosis*. Philadelphia. Blanchard and Lea. 1854.
25. Bertin, R. J. *Treatise on the Diseases of the heart and Great Vessels*. Philadelphia. Carey, Lea & Blanchard. 1833.
26. Blackall, John. Observations on the Nature and Cure of Dropsies. Philadelphia. James Webster. 1820.
27. Bowditch, Henry J. *The Young Stethoscopist / The Student's aid to Ausculation*. New York. Samuel S. & William Wood. 1848.
28. Brigham, A. *A Treatise on Epidemic Cholera*. Hartford. H. and F. J. Hunington. 1832. Including an historical account of its origin and progress, to the present period, compiled from the most authentic sources.
29. Brown, John. *The elements of medicine of John Brown, M.D., translated from the Latin, with comments and illustrations by the author*. Two volumes. London. J. Johnson. 1795.
30. Carpenter, William Benjamin. *Principles of Human Physiology, with their chief applications to psychology,*

pathology, therapeutics, hygiène, and forensic medicine.
Philadelphia. Blanchard and Lea. 1853.
31. Coxe, John Redman. *The American Dispensatory.*
Philadelphia. Thomas Dobson. 1810. Contains the
operations of pharmacy together with the natural history
of the different substances employed in medicine.
32. Denison, Charles. *Exercises and Food for Pulmonary
Invalids.* Denver. The Chain & Hardy Co. 1895.
33. Drake, Daniel., M.D. *A Practical Treatise on the History,
Prevention, and Treatment of Epidemic Cholera.*
Cincinnati. Corey and Fairbank. 1832.
34. Drake, Daniel., M.D. *Practical Essays on Medical
Education and the Medical Profession in the United
States.* Cincinnati. Roff & Young. 1832.
35. Ducamp, Theodore. *A Treatise on Retention of Urine
Caused by Strictures in the Urethra and the Means by
Which Obstructions of this Canal may be Effectually
Removed.* New York. Samuel Wood & Sons. 1827.
36. Eberle, John, M.D. *A Treatise on the Materia Medica and
Therapeutics.* Baltimore. S. & W. Meeteer. 1824.
37. Ewell, James. *The Planter's and Mariner's Medical
Companion.* Baltimore. P. Mauro. 1813. Contents:
Treating according to the most successful practice. The
diseases common to warm climates and on shipboard.
Common cases in surgery, such as fractures, dislocations
and other cases. The complaints common to women and
children.
38. Fordyce, George. Five Dissertations on Fever. Boston.
Lilly, Wait and Company. 1834.
39. Fothergill, John. *A Complete Collection of the Medical
and Philosophical Works of John Fothergill, M.D.F.R.S.
and S.A. Member of the Royal College of Physicians at
London and Edinburgh; of the Royal Medical Society at*

Paris; and of the American Philosophical Society. London. John Walker. 1781.

40. Gross, Samuel D. *The Anatomy, Physiology, and Diseases of the Bones and Joints.* Philadelphia. John Grigg. 1830.

41. Haller, Albert. *Dr. Albert Haller's Physiology.* Two volumes. London. G. Robinson. 1772. A course of lectures upon the visceral anatomy and vital economy of human bodies.

42. Holland, J. W. *Diet for the Sick.* Louisville. John P. Morton & Company. 1880.

43. Hooper, Robert. *Lexicon-Medicum.* New York. E. Bliss & E. White, 1822. A medical dictionary containing an explanation of the terms in anatomy, botany, chemistry, materia medica, midwifery, mineralogy, pharmacy, physiology, practice of physic, and surgery.

44. Keen, William W. *Health Manuals.* Philadelphia. Blakiston, Sons & Company. 1879.

45. Larrey, D. J. *Memoirs of Military Surgery: and Campaigns of the French Armies on the Rhine, in Corsica, Catalonia, Egypt, and Syria.* Baltimore. Joseph Cushing. 1814.

46. Lavoisier, Antoine Laurent. *Elements of Chemistry, in a New Systematic Order, Containing All the Modern Discoveries.* Philadelphia. Marthey Carey. 1799.

47. Lister, Joseph. *The Collected Papers of Joseph Baron Lister.* Two volumes. Oxford. Clarendon Press. 1909.

48. London Medical Society of Observation. *What to Observe at the Bed-Side and after death in Medical Cases.* Philadelphia. Blanchard and Lea. 1855.

49. Malgaigne, J. F. *A Treatise on Fractures.* Philadelphia. J. B. Lippincott & Company. 1859.

50. Mathis, Andrew. *The Mercurial Disease*. Philadelphia. Edward Parker. 1811. An inquiry into the history and nature of the disease produced in the human constitution by the use of mercury with observations on its connection with the lues venerea.
51. Morris, Henry. *Morris's Human Anatomy*. Philadelphia. P. Blakiston Son & Company. 1907.
52. Motherby, G. *A New Medical Dictionary*. London. J. Johnson. 1801.
53. Mudge, John. *A Radical and Expeditious Cure for Recent Catarrhous Cough*. London. J. G. Kaven. 1783.
54. Murray, Adolphus. *A Description of the Arteries of the Human Body*. Philadelphia. Thomas Dobson. 1810.
55. Osborn, William. *Essays on the Practice of Midwifery in Natural and Difficult Labors*. London. J. Johnson. 1795.
56. Pierson, Daniel. *Notes on Surgery / From the Lectures of Dr. Physick, Professor of Surgery in the University of Pennsylvania*. Handwritten. 1812.
57. Richardson, Benjamin Ward. *Temperance Lesson Book*. New York. National Temperance Society and Publication House. 1878.
58. Rush, Benjamin. *Medical Inquiries and Observations upon the Diseases of the Mind*. Philadelphia. Kimber & Richardson. 1812.
59. Salter, Henry Hyde. *On Asthma / Its Pathology and Treatment*. Philadelphia. Blanchard and Lea. 1864.
60. Senac, Jean Baptiste. *A Treatise on the hidden Nature and Treatment of Intermitting and Remitting Fevers*. Two volumes. Philadelphia. Kimber, Conrad and Company. 1805. Translated from the Latin, with notes, by Charles Caldwell and a recommendatory preface by Benjamin Rush.

61. Smith, Edward. *Consumption: Its Early and Remediable States*. Philadelphia. Blanchard and Lea. 1865.
62. Smith Joseph Mather. *Elements of the Etiology and Philosophy of Epidemics*. New York. J. & J. Harper. 1824.
63. Society of Physicians in London. *Medical Observations an Inquires by a Society of Physicians in London*. Vol. 1. London. William Johnston. 1757.
64. Society of Physicians in London. *Medical Observations an Inquires by a Society of Physicians in London*. Vol. 2. London. William Johnston. 1762.
65. Society of Physicians in London. *Medical Observations an Inquires by a Society of Physicians in London*. Vol. 3. London. William Johnston. 1769.
66. Society of Physicians in London. *Medical Observations an Inquires by a Society of Physicians in London*. Vol. 4. London. T. Cadell. 1771.
67. Steward, James. *A Practical Treatise on the Diseases of Children*. New York. Wiley & Putnam. 1841
68. Steward, James. *A Practical Treatise on the Diseases of Children*. New York. Harper & Brothers. 1845.
69. Todd, Robert Bentley. Clinical Lectures on Certain Diseases of the Urinary Organs and on Dropsies. Philadelphia. Blanchard and Lea. 1857.
70. Wales, Philip S. *Mechanical Therapeutics: A Practical Treatise on Surgical Apparatus, Appliances, and Elementary Operations*. Philadelphia. Henry C. Lea. 1867.
71. Warren, John. *A View of the Mercurial Practice in Febrile Diseases*. Boston. T. B. Wait and Company. 1813.

Appendix B

Publications of David Prince, M.D.

Sources: Index Catalogue Library Surgeon General Office, U.S. Army; Google Books; https//archive.org; University of Illinois Chicago Library of Health Sciences Special Collections; WorldCat.org.

BOOKS:

1. Prince, David, M.D. *Reports on Orthopedic Surgery made to the Illinois State Medical Society.* Part 1 on Telipes. Chicago. G. M. Fargus. 1864.

2. Prince, David, M.D. *Orthopedics: A Systematic Treatise upon the Prevention and Correction of Deformities.* Philadelphia. Lindsay & Blakiston. 1866.

3. Prince, David, M.D. *Plastics: A New Classification and A Brief Exposition of Plastic Surgery.* Reprinted from *Transactions of the Illinois State Medical Society.* Philadelphia. Lindsay and Blakiston. 1868.

4. Prince, David, M.D. *Plastics and Orthopedics.* Reprinted from editions of three reports made the Illinois State Medical Society on Plastic and Orthopedic Surgery in the years, respectively, 1864, 1867, 1871. Philadelphia. Lindsay and Blakiston. 1871.

5. Prince, David, M.D. *Galvano-Therapeutics.* A reprinting of two reports made to the Illinois State Medical Society, for 1867, Philadelphia. Lindsay & Blakiston. 1874.

6. Prince, David, M.D. *Palato-Plasty.* Reprinted from the *American Practitioner*, March 1876. Bound in back of

Plastics and Orthopedics. Philadelphia. Lindsay and Blakiston. 1876.

7. Prince, David, M.D. *Diseases of the Joints.* Reprinted from the American Practitioner, February 1877. Bound in the back of *Plastics and Orthopedics*, 1877. Philadelphia. Lindsay and Blakiston. 1877.
8. Prince, David, M.D. *The Management of Wounds.* 1881.
9. Prince, David, M.D, *An Aseptic Atmosphere. Club Foot. A Rectal Obturator. Palatroplasty.* 1888.

ARTICLES, REPORTS, MONOGRAPHS (A partial list):

1   Prince, David, M.D. "A Report on Fever." *The Illinois and Indiana Medical and Surgical Journal.* Vol. II, No. 1. Chicago. April 1847. 1-12. Source: University of Chicago Library of Health Sciences. Special Collections.
2   Prince, David, M.D. "Solid Ovarian Tumour, extending from Pubis to right Hypochondrium – Cured by Incision followed by Suppuration." *The American Journal of the Medical Sciences.* Series XX. Philadelphia. 1850. 267-268.
3   Prince, David, M.D. "Transposition of the Stomach and Duodenum. Concealment of the colon behind the Duodenum. Strangulation of the Colon rapidly fatal, resulting from this congenital malposition." *The American Journal of the Medical Sciences. Vol. XXV.* Philadelphia. 1853. 558-559.
4   Prince, David, M.D. "Empyema Treated by Injections." *The Chicago Medical Journal. Vol. 1. No. 3.* Chicago. March 1858. 95-96.
5   Prince, David, M.D. "Extirpation of the Parotid Gland". *The American Journal of the Medical Sciences. Vol. XL.* Philadelphia. 1860. 57-62.

6 Prince, David, M.D. "Delayed Union of Fractures, with Cases and illustrations; the Successful Employment of Malgaigne's Spike in connection with Drilling in a case which had previously resisted drilling employed by itself." *The American Journal of the Medical Sciences. Vol. 46.* Philadelphia. 1863. 313-322. (with six woodcuts.)

7 Prince, David, M.D. "Report on Orthopedic Surgery." Chicago. *Transactions of the Illinois Medical Society.* 1864.

8 Prince, David, M.D. "Plans for Exsection of the Upper End of Humerus, and for Amputation of the Arm and the Thigh, with Explanations." *The American Journal of Medical Science. Vol 49.* Philadelphia. April 1865. 304-317.

9 Prince, David, M.D. "Instruments for Facilitating Surgical Operations." *The American Journal of Medical Science. Vol 50.* Philadelphia. 1866. 147- 149.

10 Prince, David, M.D. "An Operation for the Correction of Inversion of the Ciliary Margin of the Eyelids, connected with Shortening of the Palpebral Fissure: by the Implantation behind the Outer Portion of the Upper Lid." *The American Journal of the Medical Sciences. Vol. 46. Issue 104.* Philadelphia. 1866. 381-390.

11 Prince, David, M.D. and Antisell, Thomas, M.D. "Patent Rights Among Medical Men." *The Transactions of the American Medical Association.* Vol. XVII. Philadelphia. 1866. 521-528.

12 Prince, David, M.D."Trial for Malpractice." *The Western Journal of Medicine.* Edited by Theophilus Parvin, M.D. Indianapolis. T. Parvin & Company. 1867. 202-215.

13 Prince, David, M.D. "Shall Hygiene be Taught in the Newspapers" The Medical and Surgical Reporter: A

Weekly Journal. Vol. XIX. Philadelphia. July-December 1868. 225-226.

14 Prince, David, M.D. "Galvano-Cautery for the Mouth of the Womb." *St. Louis Medical and Surgical Journal.* 1875.

15 Prince, David, M.D. "Galvano-Therapeutics." *Transactions of the Illinois State Medical Society.* Chicago. Fergus Printing Company. 1875. 70-77.

16 Prince, David, M.D. "Palatoplasty." *St. Louis Medical and Surgical Journal.* 1875.

17 Prince, David, M.D. "Upon Palato-Pasty with a new Instrument." *St. Louis Medical and Surgical Journal.* January 1875.

18 Prince, David, M.D. "Diphtheria." *St. Louis. St. Louis Medical and Surgical Journal.* 1876. A paper read before the St. Louis Medical Society in which a weak solution of iodine in perpetual spray is advocated.

19 Prince, David, M.D. "A Case of Ovariotomy." *St. Louis Medical and Surgical Journal.* 1876.

20 Prince, David, M.D. "Considerations in Relation to Diseases of the Joints." Louisville, *American Practitioner.* 1877.

21 Prince, David, M.D. "Instrument in Urono-Plasty." *Half-yearly Compendium of Medical Science.* Philadelphia. Medical Publication Office. 1877.

22 Prince, David, M.D. "Bathing, cupping, electricity, massage." Louisville. *American Practitioner.* 1878. A Comparison of the therapeutic effects of bathing, of cupping or atmospheric exhaustion, of electricity in the form of galvanism and faradism, and message, in the treatment of debilities, deformities, and chronic diseases.

23 Prince, David, M.D. "Lithotomy." *St. Louis Med. and Surgical Journal.* St. Louis. 1878.

24 Prince, David, M.D. "Sprague's Galvanometer Arranged for Therapeutic Uses." *Transactions of the Illinois State Medical Society*. Chicago. H. Wilson & Co. 1878.

25 Prince, David, M.D. "The Sanitation of Small Cities: Soil damage, sewerage and the disposal of sewage." *Transactions of the Illinois Medical Society Journal*. 1879.

26 Prince, David, M.D. "Partial Forward Dislocation of the head of the Homarus." *St. Louis Medical and Surgical Journal*. 1879.

27 Prince, David, M.D. "Management of Wounds" *St. Louis Medical and Surgical Journal*. 1881.

28 Prince, David, M.D. "Treatment of Exstrophy of the Bladder." *St. Louis Medical and Surgical Journal*.1881.

29 Prince, David, M.D. "A Rectal Obturator." *St. Louis Medical and Surgical Journal*. 1883.

30 Prince, David, M.D. "The Bead Structure, a modification of the quilled suture for palatoplasty." Brooklyn. *American Anatomy and Surgical Society*. 1883.

31 Prince, David, M.D. "Alcohol In some of its immediate surgical relations and in some of it remote effects." Monograph. 1884.

32 Prince, David, M.D. "Floating Minute Organic Matter in the Air and its Management to Prevent Disease and to mitigate or control it, with a new Device for Atmospheric Purification." *St. Louis Medical and Surgical Journal*. 1885.

33 Prince, David, M.D. "Erysipelas and other Septic and infectious Diseases Incident to Injuries and Surgical Operations Prevented by a Method of Atmospheric Purification." Louisville. *American Practitioner*. 1886.

34 Prince, David, M.D. "Wounds: Their Aseptic and antiseptic Management." Philadelphia. *Transactions of the American Surgical Association.* 1887.

35 Prince, David, M.D. "Pelvic and Abdominal Drainage." *The Transactions of the American Medical Association.* 1888.

36 Prince, David, M.D. "The Hedge Thorn Poison." Chicago. *Transactions of the Illinois Medical Society Journal.* 1889.

Appendix C

"A Great Physician"

The Eulogy of David Prince by Illinois College President Edward A. Tanner delivered at Jacksonville Congregational Church December 22, 1889.

With profound respect, with grateful affection, and with an indescribable sense of loneliness, do I rise to speak beside the coffin of one, who has been to me health in sickness, rest in weariness and good cheer amid multiplied anxieties.

There is no other relation like that to the trusted physician, who has been in the house when the angel of life has entered, or when the angel of death, with his black wings, has blown out the light of the fireside.

It is almost forty years since in boyhood I first heard of this then young surgeon's fame, but for only half of that period has there been a familiar home acquaintance. That word, familiar, sounds strangely to many. Say they, any other adjective would be more appropriate in speaking of the quiet, silent, reserved, sometimes brusque and distant David Prince, whom we have nevertheless held in the highest esteem. I used to think so. Much as I admired the man's professional skill and blunt sincerity, there was great constraint in his society.

One day back in the seventies, we happened to be in the same room together alone. There was no escape. We sat in silence half an hour. We looked vacantly at each other. Then both began to smile. Then both burst into a laugh. Then the ice broke up and went out, as it does in the river in early spring. And since then, the current of conversation has always been open between us two, till now.

One night, a dozen years ago, we sat up till into the small hours of the morning, discussing revealed religion and, especially, the revelation of God in Christ. His words and bearing were earnest and reverent. Our creeds were in part concurrent, in part divergent, and we bade each other good-bye, saying that, whichever was right and whichever was wrong, if we could preserve that same spirit of patient docility, we should at length be guided to a knowledge of all essential truth. Since then, we have had no long formal talk on such questions, and it is not "wise to speculate upon them in this presence." I think that if our departed friend could speak, this is what he would wish to say.

Doctor David Prince was an enthusiast in his profession. It is peculiarly the profession of the family. Sons and son-in-law all follow in his footsteps. Large numbers of the medical fraternity from the region have come to do honor to his memory today. In view of these facts, it is appropriate that, here in the house of him who was known as the Great Physician, we should speak briefly of this high calling. I believe that what may be said, would have the cordial approbation of him who is speechless on earth forever.

There is more to fear from turning the back upon scientific research, or from approaching it with fear and trembling, than from engaging in it patiently and exhaustively, in the candid spirit of Doctor David Prince, who was ready to abandon any darling hypothesis, the moment it was proved false to facts.

Though skeptical in his tendencies, he became so impressed with the evidences of adaptation and design that were forced upon him, by his constant examination of the frame work of the body, that he was brought at last to subscribe, most reverently, to the doctrine of an omnipotent and omniscient Creator. At the foot of some dangerous plants, you may find growing nature's own remedy for any harm which those plants may inflict. So, while there are dangers connected with your beneficent vocation the blessed antidote is never far away.

I wish that it were proper for me to repeat here a story that I heard last night, concerning the tender and reassuring way in which this man, so strong and rugged, led a timid and shrinking woman down till the cold waters touched her feet, and her lips were ready for the song which the immortals sing. I wish that it were proper to make articulate here the dumb testimony which is locked up in the breasts of a great multitude of the poor, both the deserving and the undeserving, (for his sympathies were so free that he could not discriminate), whom he visited in sickness, without thought of compensation. But that is not necessary, for it is familiar knowledge to you all, and the departed himself would protest against such recitals.

There has been one hard feature of Doctor Prince's professional life, about which he never complained, but which ought to be mentioned. It was caused by his very eminence as a surgeon. He has had to deal with more desperate cases than any other doctor in Central Illinois. Besides the natural proportion of such in his own vicinity, it has long been the custom of general practitioners, who have not made surgery a specialty, when ordinary measures have failed, to summon this veteran, who, it is no discredit to younger men to say, has long held the first rank here as a surgeon. In dealing with so many forlorn hopes, heroic expedients have often been necessary, and, occasionally, good but thoughtless people, ignorant of the facts, have been unjust in their judgment of this man of steady nerve, and cunning hand, and loving heart.

This is mentioned to emphasize the spirit with which such misapprehensions have been borne. It is worthy of admiration and of imitation by all public men. Doctor Prince never went about making explanations and excuses. He did not rush into the papers to air his personal grievances, real or imaginary; but with quiet dignity threw himself back upon his character, content to let that take care of his reputation. In this view, would it be any flattery to say, that the manliest man among us died the other night? Such an affirmation is not made, but the question may stimulate beneficial self-examination.

In the public library and reading room, many books and periodicals inscribed with the name of Doctor David Prince, bear silent witness to his thoughtfulness for those of both sexes and of all ages, who are largely indebted to such philanthropic enterprises for enlightenment. It was a happy suggestion at the meeting last night, that the city should honor herself, by making that public library a memorial of him who loved the people. Who can take the place of Doctor David Prince in the affections of the pupils and teachers of our common schools?

No one else has been more zealous in the support of a high school for the sons and daughters of those unable to pay the cost of tuition for advanced instruction. The institutions for the education of the blind, and of the deaf and dumb, have always found him eager to aid in magnifying their beneficent work. The commercial school has prized his kindly appreciation of its efforts to promote system and efficiency in business methods. Our female seminaries have lost one of their best friends, an enthusiastic advocate of the highest learning for woman.

Illinois College has enjoyed in him a wise and liberal counsellor. For years there has not been formed for her welfare a single plan, which has not had his sympathy, verbal and pecuniary. More than once has he said: " Come to me whenever there is a project on foot to render the college a greater blessing." More than once has he sought an opportunity to make a generous donation before he was approached on the subject. How many citizens are there left in Jacksonville who cherish for all our institutions of learning an interest so discriminating and comprehensive, as did the beloved physician of the great heart and the liberal hand?

Fond father, tender husband, loyal brother, friend never false, shining light in an illustrious profession, honor to the city, noble figure in the commonwealth, model American citizen, lover of every creature that beareth the image of God, Farewell.

Source: Tanner, Edward Allen, D.D. "A Great Physician." *Baccalaureate and Other Sermons, and Addresses.* Chicago and New York. Fleming H. Revell Company. 1892. (Edited for length)

Bibliography

BOOKS

1. Adams, George Worthington. *Doctors in Blue / The Medical History of the Union Army in The Civil War.* Baton Rouge: Louisiana State University Press, 1952.
2. Baldwin, Theron. *Historical sketch of the origin, progress, and wants, of Illinois College.* New York. John T. West, Printer. 1832.
3. Ball, James Moores, M.D. *The Sack-'Em-Up Men.* London. Oliver and Boyd. 1928.
4. Barwick, Gary Jack and Kay, Betty Carlson. *Images of American Jacksonville Illinois The Traditions Continue.* Charleston, Arcadia Publishing. 1999.
5. Bateman, Newton; Selby, Paul and Currey, J. Seymour. *Historical Encyclopedia of Illinois.* Chicago. Munsell Publishing Company. 1925.
6. Black, Carl E., M.D. and Bessie M. *From Pioneer to Scientist – The Life Story of Greene Vardiman Black.* Saint Paul, MN. Bruce Publishing Company. 1940.
7. *Brief History of the Charitable Institutions of the State of Illinois.* Committee on the State Charitable Institutions of the Illinois Board of World's Fair Commissioners. Chicago. John Morris Company, Printer. 118 Monroe Street. Chicago. 1893.
8. Brown, Thomas J. *Dorothea Dix New England Reformer.* Cambridge. Harvard University Press. 1998.
9. Carriel, Mary Turner. *The Life of Jonathan Baldwin Turner.* 1911.

10. Chandler, Josephine Craven. *Dr. Charles Chandler, his place in the American scene.* Springfield, IL. Phillips Bros. Printers. 1932.
11. *Collected Works of Abraham Lincoln. Volume 4. Lincoln, Abraham, 1809-1865.* New Brunswick, N.J.: Rutgers University Press. Ann Arbor, Michigan: University of Michigan Digital Library Production Services. 1953.
12. Crellin, John N. *Medical Care in Pioneer Illinois.* Springfield. Pearson Museum. Southern Illinois University Foundation. 1982.
13. Cunningham, H. H. *Doctors in Gray.* Baton Rouge. Louisiana State University Press. 1958.
14. Davis, David J., Editor. *History of Medical Practice in Illinois Vol. II: 1850-1900.* Chicago. The Illinois State Medical Society. The Lakeside Press, R. R. Donnelley & Sons. 1955.
15. Denney, Robert E. *Civil War Medicine.* New York. Sterling Publishing Company, Inc. 1995.
16. Denney, Robert E. *Civil War Prisons & Escapes.* New York. Sterling Publishing Co., Inc. 1993.
17. Donnelley, Lloyd & Company. *History of Morgan County, Illinois: its past and present.* Chicago. 1878.
18. Dorrance, George Morris. *The Operative Story of Cleft Palate.* Philadelphia. W. B. Saunders Company. 1933. Northern Illinois University. DeKalb, IL.
19. Doyle, Don Harrison. *Chaos and Community in a Frontier Town: Jacksonville, Illinois, 1825-1860.* PhD Thesis/dissertation. Northwestern University. Main Library. Evanston, Illinois. Film 5599. 1973.
20. Doyle, Don Harrison. *The Social Order of a Frontier Community Jacksonville, Illinois 1825-70.* Urbana. University of Illinois Press. 1978.

21. Drake, Daniel, M.D. *Narrative of the Rise and Fall of the Medical College of Ohio.* Looker & Reynolds. Cincinnati. 1822.
22. Drake, Daniel, M.D. *Practical Essays on Medical Education and the Medical Profession in the United States.* Hoff & Young. Cincinnati. 1832.
23. Eames, Charles M. *Historic Morgan and Classic Jacksonville.* 1884-'85. The Daily Journal steam job printing office, Jacksonville, IL. 1885.
24. Freemon, Frank R. *Gangrene and Glory.* Madison, N.J. Fairleigh Dickinson University Press. c1998.
25. Gerberding, G. H. *Life and Letters of W. A. Passavant, D. D.* Greenville, PA. The Young Lutheran Co. 1906.
26. Gross, Samuel D., M.D. *Autobiography of Samuel D. Gross, M.D.* Philadelphia. George Barrie, Publisher. 1887.
27. Heinl, Frank J. "An Epitome of Jacksonville History to 1875." *Jacksonville Centennial Commission 1825-1925.* Jacksonville. 1925.
28. Heinl, Frank J. "Jacksonville and Morgan County an Historical Review." *Journal of the Illinois State Historical Society (1908-1984). Vol. 18, No.1. Jacksonville Centennial. April 1925.* 5-38. Champaign-Urbana, University of Illinois Press.URL: http://www.jstor.org/stable/40187246. Accessed: 25/3/2012.
29. *History of Morgan County: Its Past and Present.* Donnelly, Lloyd & Company. 1878.
30. Iacobbo, Karen and Michael Iacobbo. *Vegetarian America.* Westport, CT. 2004.
31. Juettner, Otto, A.M., M.D. *Daniel Drake and His Followers.* Cincinnati. Harvey Publishing Company. 1909.

32. Kampmeier, Otto F. "History of the Anatomy Laws in Illinois during the 19th Century." *History of Medical Practice in Illinois Vol. II: 1850-1900*. Chicago. The Illinois State Medical Society. The Lakeside Press, R. R. Donnelley & Sons. 1955. Pages 361-402.

33. Kampmeier, Otto F. "Medical Libraries in Illinois Preceding 1900." *History of Medical Practice in Illinois Vol. II: 1850-1900*. Chicago. The Illinois State Medical Society. The Lakeside Press, R. R. Donnelley & Sons. 1955. Pages 434-472.

34. Larrey, Baron Dominique Jean. *Observations on Wounds, and Their Complications by Erysipelas, Gangrene and Tetanus, and on the Principal Diseases and Injuries of the Head, Ear, and Eye*. Philadelphia. Key, Mielke & Biddle. 1832. Translated from the French by E. F. Rivinus, M.D. (Illinois College Schewe Library).

35. Lightner, David L. *Asylum, Prison, and Poorhouse / The Writings and Reform Work of Dorothea Dix in Illinois*. Carbondale and Edwardsville. Southern Illinois University Press. 1999.

36. Mussey, Reuben D., M.D. *Health: Its Friends and Its Foes*. Boston. Gould and Lincoln. 1862.

37. O'Donnell, Thomas C. *Tip of the Hill*. Booneville, New York. Black River Books. 1953.

38. Peck, J. M. *A Gazetteer of Illinois, 2nd Edition*. Philadelphia. Gregg & Elliot. 1837.

39. Perret, Geoffrey. *Lincoln's War*. New York. Random House. 2004.

40. Prince, Arthur E. *Clinical Notes of the David Prince Sanitorium*. Springfield, Illinois. 1907.

41. Prince, David, M.D. *Orthopedics: A Systematic Treatise Upon the Prevention and Correction of Deformities*. Philadelphia. Lindsay & Blackiston. 1866.

42. Prince, David, M.D. *Plastics and orthopedics: being editions of three reports made to the Illinois State Medical Society, in the years, respectively, 1864, 1867 & 187.* Philadelphia. Lindsay and Blakston. 1871. [Also, referenced following the title page: Jacksonville, IL. Deaf and Dumb Steam Press.]

43. Prince, David, M.D. *Plastics: A New Classification and a Brief Exposition of Plastic Surgery.* Philadelphia. Lindsay and Blakiston. 1868. A reprint from a report in the Transactions of the Illinois State Medical Society for 1867.

44. Rammelkamp, Charles Henry. *Illinois College A Centennial History 1829-1929.* New Haven: Yale University Press, 1928.

45. Rawlings, Isaac D. *The Rise and Fall of Disease in Illinois. Vol.1 and 2.* Springfield, IL: Illinois State Department of Public Health, 1927.

46. Rocco, Fiammetta. *The Miraculous Fever Tree/ Malaria and the Quest for a Cure that changed the World.* New York. Harper Collins. 2003.

47. Rush, Benjamin, M.D. *Medical Inquires and Observations: containing an account of the Yellow Fever, as it appeared in Philadelphia in 1797, and Observations upon the nature and Cure of the gout, and Hydrophobia.* Philadelphia. Budd and Bartram. 1798.

48. Sappol, Michael. *A Traffic of Dead Bodies.* Princeton and Oxford: Princeton University Press, 2002.

49. Sears, Stephen W. *To the Gates of Richmond: The Peninsula Campaign.* New York. Ticknor & Fields. 1992.

50. Shastid, Thomas Hall, M.D., *My Second Life and Autobiography*, Ann Arbor, George Wahr, publisher to the University of Michigan, 1944.

51. Spalding, Dr. James Alfred. *Dr. Lyman Spalding*. Boston. W.M. Leonard, Publisher. 1916.
52. Stillé, Charles J. *History of the United States Sanitary Commission*. Philadelphia. J. B. Lippincott & Co. 1866.
53. Sturtevant, Julian M. *An Autobiography*. Chicago. Fleming H. Revell Company. 1896.
54. Swiderski, Richard M. *Calomel in America / Mercurial Panacea, War, Song and Ghosts*. Boca Raton. Brown Walker Press. 2009.
55. Weaver, George Howlett. *Beginnings of Medical Education in and near Chicago / The institutions and the men*. Chicago. Press of the American Medical Association. Reprinted from the *Proceedings of the Institute of Medicine of Chicago 1925, Vol. 5* and the *Bulletin of the Society of Medical History of Chicago 1925*, Vol. 3.
56. Yeager, Iver F. *Julian M Sturtevant 1805 – 1886 president of Illinois College, Ardent Churchman, Reflective Author*. Jacksonville, Illinois. The Trustees of Illinois College. 1999.
57. Zeuch, Lucius H., M.D. *History of Medical Practice in Illinois. Vol. I Preceding 1850*. Chicago. Book Press. 1927.

ARTICLES

1. "Abolitionism 1830-1850/The Pro-slavery Riot in Cincinnati." http://utc.iath.virginia.edu/abolitn/mobhp.html.
2. Black, Carl E., M.D. "A Pioneer Medical School." *Illinois Medical Journal*.1-25. January 1913.
3. Black, Carl E., M.D. "Illinois' First Medical School." *Bulletin of Medical History of Chicago, Vol. 1, No. 3*. Chicago. March 1913.

4. Black, Carl E. M.D. "Medical Practice in Illinois Before Hard Roads." *Bulletin of the Society of Medical History of Chicago.* June 1946.

5. Black, Carl E., M.D. *The Morgan County Medical Society 1867-1917.* Jacksonville, IL, 1917.

6. Black, Carl E., M.D. "Origin of Our State Charitable Institutions." *Journal of the Illinois State Historical Society (1908-1984).* Vol. 18, No. 1, Jacksonville Centennial Number (Apr.,1925), pp175-194. University of Illinois Press on behalf of the Illinois State Historical Society.

7. *Brief History of the Charitable Institutions of the State of Illinois.* Committee on State Charitable Institutions of the Illinois Board of World's Fair Commissioners. Chicago. John Morris Company, Printer, 118 and 120 Monroe Street, Chicago. 1893.

8. Drennan, Marjorie Black. "Memoir." Interview by Barbara Gross, 1974. Archives/Special Collections LIB 144. University of Illinois at Springfield. Springfield IL.

9. Duncan, Elizabeth. *Diary of Mrs. Joseph Duncan.* Journal of the Illinois State Historical Society.

10. Goldwyn, Robert M., M.D. and Ossoff, Robert H. "David Prince, 1816-1890." *Journal of American Society of Plastic Surgeons. Plastic and Reconstructive Surgery.* June 1994 vol. 93, Issue 7. 1514-1519.

11. Kilham, John. "John Kilham Letter of 1831." *Quarterly.* Jacksonville Area Genealogical and Historical Society, June 2012. Pages 44-46.

12. Mead, Edward, M.D. "An Appeal in Behalf of the Insane." *The American Psychological Journal*, Vol. 5. Cincinnati. September 1853.

13. "Medical School of Fairfield." *The Western Journal, Vol. V, No. 1*. Cincinnati. Edited and Published by the medical faculty of the Cincinnati College. Cincinnati Hospital. July 1837. 144.

14. Goldwyn, Robert M., M.D. and Ossoff, Robert H. "David Prince, 1816-1890." *Journal of American Society of Plastic Surgeons. Plastic and Reconstructive Surgery.* June 1994 vol. 93, Issue 7. 1514-1519.

15. Lightner, David L. *Asylum, Prison, and Poorhouse / The Writings and Reform Work of Dorothea Dix in Illinois.* Carbondale and Edwardsville. Southern Illinois University Press. 1999.

16. Norbury, Frank B. M.D. "*David Prince/ A Pioneer in Surgical Therapeutics in Central Illinois.* Paper prepared for the dedication of The Pearson Museum, Southern Illinois University School of Medicine. Springfield. November 15, 1980.

17. Norbury, Frank B., M.D. *Dorothea Dix and the Founding of Illinois' First Mental Hospital.* Journal of the Illinois State Historical Society 92:1. Spring 1999.

18. Prince, David, M.D." Trial for Malpractice. "*The Western Journal of Medicine.* Edited by Theophilus Parvin, M.D. Indianapolis. T. Parvin & Company. 1867.

19. Palmer, John McAuley. *The Bench and the Bar of Illinois Historical and Reminiscent.* Chicago. The Lewis Publishing Company. 1899.

20. Peck, J. M., *A Gazetteer of Illinois*, 2nd Edition, Philadelphia, Grigg & Elliot, 1837.

21. Pearson, Emmet F., M.D. "John F. Snyder, M.D. / A Pioneer Illinois Physician and Scholar." *Illinois Medical*

Journal. Nov 174 (5) 304-7 Nov. (Advocate Lutheran General Hospital Library, Park Ridge, IL).

22. *Vegetarian Messenger, The.* London. J.M. Burton and Company, steam press. 1852.

23. Velek, Miroslav, M.D. "Jacksonville State Hospital: The First Psychiatric Hospital in Illinois." *Pearson Museum monograph series, no.82/4.* Department of Medical Humanities, Southern Illinois University, School of Medicine, 1982. Springfield, IL.

58. Weaver, George Howlett. "Edward Mead, M.D. the pioneer neuropsychiatrist of Illinois." *Bulletin of Society of Medical History of Illinois.* Vol. 111. Chicago. 1924. pp 279-292. Newberry Library.

59. Willard, Samuel. "Personal Reminiscences of Life in Illinois – 1830 to 1850." *Transactions of the Illinois State Historical Society* 11 (1906): 73-87. 1906.

UNPUBLISHED ARTICLES

1. Black, Carl E. "David Prince." Unpublished. Read before the Western Surgical Association, Kansas City, MO. December 1936. Jacksonville (IL) Public Library Special Collections.

2. Kampmeier, Otto F. *The Story of Human Anatomy in Illinois During the Nineteenth Century. Unpublished Papers.* Incomplete manuscript. Undated. University of Illinois Chicago. Health Sciences Special Collection. Series 016/19/20/02-Box 7 of 9.

3. Prince, Arthur E. M. D. "Clinical Notes of The David Prince Sanitarium for the Eye, Ear, Nose and Throat." Springfield, Illinois. 1907.

CPSIA information can be obtained
at www.ICGtesting.com
Printed in the USA
LVHW110409020921
696501LV00001B/5

9 781647 194888